情景英语教程

Situational English

肖德钧 王正华/主　编

周建惠/主　审

方玉琴 檀祝平 杨建英 郭靖/副主编

天津大学出版社
TIANJIN UNIVERSITY PRESS

内容提要

　　《情景英语教程》根据《高职高专教育英语课程教学基本要求》和英语教学改革的成果编写而成。本教材将高职公共英语课程所学的语言知识、技能在真实或模拟的日常生活场景中熟练运用，培养学生综合运用英语的能力和学生分析问题、解决问题、合作交流等核心能力。教材选取了日常生活中常用的 15 个生活场景作为学生的学习训练项目，每个项目又包含 7～8 个情景和多个任务，倡导情景和任务型教学模式。

　　本教材既可用于高职公共英语理论教学体系中的提高阶段，即作为语言综合运用能力模块课程精品教材，也可作为高职公共英语实践教学体系中的实训课程教材。本教程还是江苏省教育厅高等成人教育精品课程《实用英语》的配套教材，供高等成人院校的学生使用。

图书在版编目(CIP)数据

　　情景英语教程/肖德钧，王正华主编．—天津：天津大学
出版社，2010.9
　　ISBN 978-7-5618-3681-1

　　Ⅰ.①情…　Ⅱ.①肖…②王…　Ⅲ.①英语—高等学校：
技术学校—教材　Ⅳ.①H31

　　中国版本图书馆 CIP 数据核字(2010)第 166412 号

出版发行	天津大学出版社
出 版 人	杨欢
地　　址	天津市卫津路 92 号天津大学内(邮编：300072)
电　　话	发行部：022-27403647　邮购部：022-27402742
网　　址	www.tjup.com
印　　刷	天津泰宇印务有限公司
经　　销	全国各地新华书店
开　　本	169mm×239mm
印　　张	16
字　　数	388 千
版　　次	2010 年 9 月第 1 版
印　　次	2010 年 9 月第 1 次
印　　数	1—3000
定　　价	30.00 元

前言

Preface

目前在高职高专的英语教材中,真正把公共英语和专业英语很好地衔接或融合的教材很少,而高职公共英语课程实践教学中的实训教材更是空白,而情景英语在这两个方面对英语教材建设就起到了加快发展和填补空白的作用。

《情景英语教程》蕴涵了人本主义和建构主义理论的思想,它突破了传统教材的结构与模式,"以学生为中心、以情景为环境、以任务为驱动",让学生自主建构知识,体现了英语教学中知识、能力和人文素质的三维目标。教材所鼓励的教学模式和策略与国际上的英语课程教材主流思想基本吻合,同时兼顾了以汉语为母语的课堂的实际教学情况和特点。教材的取材和项目话题的选择能够充分注意实用性、交际性和多样性;教材内容贴近学生的生活实际,编排形式生动活泼、可读性很强。教材充分考虑了学生的年龄和心理特征,也考虑到语言教学的特色。

1. 内容简介

《情景英语教程》根据《高职高专教育英语课程教学基本要求》和英语教学改革的成果编写而成。本教程是中国职教学会 2009－2010 年度高职教育英语类教学改革与建设政策指导项目及常州科教城 2009 年度院校科研基金项目《基于能力和素质发展的高职英语教学模式和评价方案研究》的主要研究成果之一。本教材将高职公共英语课程所学的知识、技能在真实或模拟的日常生活场景中熟练运用,强化学生在一般生活环境下听、说、读、写、译五个方面的基本技能,培养学生综合运用英语进行沟通的能力,培养学生分析问题、解决问题、合作交流与创新意识等核心能力。使学生在原有英语水平的基础上,进一步提高英语水平,学习行业英语,掌握本专业和专业相关技术领域职业岗位所需的英语技能和实用综合能力,有效地为职业领域服务打下基础。

编写组选取了日常生活中常用的 15 个生活场景作为学生的学习训练项目,每个项目又包含 7～8 个情景和多个任务,倡导情景和任务型教学模式。让学生在教师的指导下,通过感知、体验、实践、合作等方式参与课堂活动,调动教师和学生两个方面的积极性,真正体现学生的主体地位,发挥教师的主导作用,改变了传统的教学模式和学生学习方式。

每个项目的结构如下:

(1)能力目标

Competence Objectives

(2)热身活动

Warm-up Activities

（3）导入情景

Situation One（Discussing）

（4）听力情景

Situation Two（🔊Listening）

Situation Three（🔊Listening）

Situation Four（🔊Listening）

（5）口语情景

Situation Five（👄Speaking）

或 Situation Six（👄Speaking）

（6）阅读情景

Situation Six（📖Reading）

或 Situation Seven（📖Reading）

（7）写作情景

Situation Seven（✒Writing）

或 Situation Eight（✒Writing）

（8）自我评价

Self-evaluation

2. 编写原则和特色

（1）以人为本，因材施教

教材本着"以人为本、承认差异、发展个性、着眼未来"的原则，在目标设定、教材编写、课程评价和教学资源的开发等方面都突出"以学生为主体"的思想，尊重学生的个体差异，创设与学生实际生活息息相关的英语学习场景和情景，融"教、学、做"为一体，从而真正提高学生语言运用能力和学生职业核心能力。

（2）基于日常生活场景，以"项目—情景—任务"的形式建构教材的内容框架

以职业功能为主线、以日常生活过程为导向、以项目为载体、以情景为语言环境、将任务训练贯穿于教学全过程。本教材以培养学生的英语实际应用能力为目标，将职业能力和日常生活中所需要的内容融入课程教材中训练。

（3）教材突出"实用为主、够用为度"，培养学生语言综合运用能力

根据《高职高专教育英语课程教学基本要求》，教材本着"实用为主、够用为度"的原则，在编写中正确处理听、说、读、写、译之间的关系，在2～3节的教学时间内，教师引导学生通过合作、探究等方式用英语完成单个场景（项目）、多个情景下的多个语言任务，在宽松的氛围中使学生羞于开口的心理障碍消失，学生的听说能力和语言实际运用能力得到训练和培养，从而为社会培养高素质高技能的应用型人才服务。

3. 编写队伍

《情景英语教程》由常州轻工职业技术学院基础部英语教研室编写，肖德钧、王正

华担任主编,周建惠担任主审,方玉琴、檀祝平、杨建英、郭靖担任副主编。具体编写分工如下:肖德钧编写了项目13的教材、答案、词汇和听力材料;王正华编写了项目6的教材、答案、词汇和听力材料;周建惠编写了项目14的教材、答案、词汇和听力材料;方玉琴编写了项目1的教材、答案、词汇和听力材料;檀祝平编写了项目15的教材、答案、词汇和听力材料;杨建英编写了项目12的教材、答案、词汇和听力材料;郭靖编写了项目11的教材、答案、词汇和听力材料;熊薇编写了项目10的教材、答案、词汇和听力材料;颜华云编写了项目5的教材、答案、词汇和听力材料;谢艳红编写了项目3的教材、答案、词汇和听力材料;汤慧编写了项目8的教材、答案、词汇和听力材料;周娟编写了项目9的教材、答案、词汇和听力材料;王良柱编写了项目7的教材、答案、词汇和听力材料;曾艳编写了项目2的教材、答案、词汇和听力材料;周雅菊编写了项目4的教材、答案、词汇和听力材料。感谢在本书的编写和出版过程中天津大学出版社给予的帮助和大力支持,同时要感谢基础部主任冯宁教授的大力支持和帮助。

由于编者水平有限,加之时间仓促,书中难免存在一些缺点和错误,恳请专家和广大读者批评指正。

情景英语编写组

2010 年 6 月

Contents

Item One   Interpersonal Communication

Competence Objectives

1. Students can know communication ways.
2. Students can communicate with others in daily life situation.
3. Students can talk about their own weekend activities.
4. Students can understand the importance of communication.
5. Students can write a greeting card and a name card.

Warm-up Activities

Look through the following pictures, and know more about the importance of communication in the world, and then talk about your favorite communication way.

Nice to meet you!

Communication between the dogs:

The communication ways：

Situation One（Discussing）

After reading the pictures，please discuss the following questions.

1. What can you see in the pictures?

2. What do you think of the Internet? What has the Internet brought to us?

3. Talk about the communication ways.

Situation Two (Listening)

Situation: Two strangers met after a conference, they introduced themselves to each other.

Task: **Listen to the conversation carefully, and then answer the questions. The conversation will be spoken twice.**

1. Where were the speakers a moment ago?

2. What is the man's last name?

3. Which department does the woman work in?

Situation Three (Listening)

Situation: A tour guide will tell the tourists something about the plan and arrangement for the tour.

Task: **You will hear the short passage with some words or phrases missing. The passage will be read twice. After the second reading, you are required to put the missing words or phrases in the blanks according to what you have heard. Now the passage will begin.**

Good evening, everyone. Welcome to our city. You will stay at the Garden Hotel tonight. I hope you'll have a good rest.

Tomorrow,   1   is served at 7:00 A. M. We'll start off at 7:45 A. M. to visit the Shanghai Radio and TV   2   . And then we'll go to visit the Shanghai   3   and Technology Museum and have lunch there. In the afternoon, at about four, we'll go to the Jinmao Building. It is the   4   building in Shanghai. In the evening we'll enjoy the beautiful   5   along the Huangpu River by ship.

Situation Four (Listening)

Situation: Caddy and Miss Fang are good friends in America, something in daily life happened between them.

Task: **Listen to the short passage and answer the following questions. The passage will be repeated twice. Before you listen, learn the following words and expressions.**

```
              Words & Expressions
secretary   文秘,秘书          apartment   一套公寓房间
impatient   不耐烦的,急躁的      puzzled   困惑的
unwilling to answer   不愿意回答
```

1. What was Caddy's job?

2. Where did Caddy come from?

3. Why didn't Miss Fang invite Caddy to her apartment?

4. What did Fang and Caddy usually do at weekends?

5. What was Caddy's attitude towards Fang recently?

Situation Five (⟺Speaking)

Situation 1: You want to have a trip to Suzhou, so you phone to a tourist agency for more information.

Situation 2: The weekend is coming, you want to spend the weekend with your good friend. So you make a telephone to your friend about the weekend activities.

Task: Make up dialogues and then act out them before the class. The following functional sentences will help you.

1. I'm afraid I must be leaving now. /I think it's time for us to leave now.

2. It's very kind of you to...

3. I wish you good luck/success!

4. Is there anything else I can do for you?

5. Are you/Will you be free this afternoon /evening/tomorrow?

6. Shall we meet at 4:30 at...?

7. Yes, that's all right. /Yes, I'll be free then.

8. Will you come to...? / Would you like to...? /I'd like to invite you to...

9. Yes, I'd love to... / Yes, it's very kind/ nice of you.

10. I'd love to, but...

Situation Six (⌂Reading)

Situation: We all know we are living in the communication world, communication is everywhere, so it is very important in our life. Let's read the following passage and know how important the communication is. Answer the two questions before getting into the passage.

1. How often do you keep in touch with your friends?

2. What do you think of the interpersonal communication? What about the communication between the other living things?

Task：Read the following passage first, try to get the main idea of the passage and then finish the tasks.

The Importance of Communication

A man and his wife were having some problems at home and were giving each other the silent **treatment**(对待,处理).

The next week, the man realized that he would need his wife to wake him at 5:00 A. M. for an early morning business flight to Chicago. Not wanting to be the first to break the silence, he wrote on a piece of paper, "Please wake me at 5:00 A. M. ".

The next morning the man woke up, only to discover it was 9:00 A. M. and that he had missed his flight. **Furious** (狂怒的,猛烈的), he was about to go and see why his wife hadn't awakened him, when he noticed a piece of paper by the bed. The paper said, "It is 5:00 A. M. Wake up. "

Communication — such a vital part of keeping marriages healthy! The greatest of problems can be solved with good communication. Even the smallest of problems can be **insurmountable**(不能克服的,难以对付的)without it!

Remember when you were dating? You spent a lot of time talking to each other. You could spend hours on the phone at a time, sharing your opinions and your preferences, or just talking about what's going on. But when you get married, you get to know each other, and you tend to quit talking, and even worse, you tend to quit listening.

Strong families communicate often. They talk about anything and everything. They also listen to each other. If a member of the family isn't communicating, they find out why. "What's the problem? Let's talk it out, let's solve the difficulty. "

The world we are living in is amazing. There are countless living things. How can they live **harmoniously** (和谐地)? The answer is also communication.

Communication, of course, doesn't need to be in words. We can talk to each other by a smile, a **frown** (皱眉), a shrug of our shoulders, and a gesture with our hands. Shaking hands is a very common gesture, which is performed both on **initial** (开始的)greeting and departure. We know that birds and animals use a whole vocabulary of songs, sounds and movements. Bees dance their signals, flying in certain pattern that tell other bees where to find **nectar**(花蜜) of honey.

Can plants talk? Yes—but not in words. We have reasons to believe that trees do communicate with each other. Researcher learned some surprising things that a willow tree attacked by **caterpillars**(毛虫) could change the chemistry of its leaves and made them taste so awful that the caterpillars stopped eating them. More astonishing, the tree could send out special signal **stimulating**(刺激) its neighbors!

Communication is so important in the nature world. As human beings we should communicate with each other to make the earth peaceful and be willing to talk. Be willing to listen. And, perhaps most importantly, make time for both. In our busy world where everybody is running in different directions all at the same time, we need to make time to be with each other and communicate. Pleasant words are like a **honey-comb**(蜂窝), sweetness to the soul and health to the bones.

Task 1:Getting a message.

After reading the passage, decide whether the following statements are true (T) or false(F).

1. A man and his wife were having some troubles at home and were not speaking to each other.

2. The man realized that he would need his wife's help, so he will be the first to break the silence.

3. When he noticed a piece of paper saying, "It is 5:00 A. M. Wake up. " by the bed, he was very crazy and angry.

4. The smallest of problems can be overcome with no communication.

5. Getting married, everyone is willing to quit talking, and even worse, to quit listening.

6. It is communication that makes countless living things live harmoniously.

7. Not all the communication needs to be in words.

8. Researcher was very surprised to learn that a willow tree attacked by caterpillars could send out special signal to its neighbors.

9. Human beings should communicate with each other to make the earth peaceful and be willing to help the animals.

10. Pleasant words can make people happy and healthy.

Task 2:Skimming and scanning.

Scan the passage and write down the key sentences of the following passages.

1. A man and his wife were having some problems at home and were giving each other the silent treatment.

The next week, the man realized that he would need his wife to wake him at 5:00 A. M. for an early morning business flight to Chicago. Not wanting to be the first to break the silence, he wrote on a piece of paper, "Please wake me at 5:00 A. M. ".

The next morning the man woke up, only to discover it was 9:00 A. M. and that he had missed his flight. Furious, he was about to go and see why his wife hadn't awakened him, when he noticed a piece of paper by the bed. The paper said, "It is 5:00 A. M. Wake up. "

Communication — such a vital part of keeping marriages healthy! The greatest of problems can be solved with good communication. Even the smallest of problems can be insurmountable without it!

What is the topic sentence of the above passage?

_____

2. The world we are living in is amazing. There are countless living things. How can they live harmoniously? The answer is also communication.

Communication, of course, doesn't need to be in words. We can talk to each other by a smile, a frown, a shrug of our shoulders, and a gesture with our hands. Shaking hands is a very common gesture, which is performed both on initial greeting and departure. We know that birds and animals use a whole vocabulary of songs, sounds, and movements. Bees dance their signals, flying in certain pattern that tell other bees where to find nectar of honey.

Can plants talk? Yes—but not in words. We have reasons to believe that trees do communicate with each other. Researcher learned some surprising things that a willow tree attacked by caterpillars could change the chemistry of its leaves and made them taste so awful that the caterpillars stopped eating them. More astonishing, the tree could send out special signal stimulating its neighbors!

What is the topic sentence of the above passage?

_____

Task 3:Translate the following sentences into English.
1. 通过眼睛来交流会更加有效。
2. 讲话前正视你的观众并作短暂停留可以帮助你留给观众良好的印象。
3. 整个讲演的过程你都应该与观众保持目光的交流。
4. 如果你只顾自己说,他们就会有被忽视的感觉,于是无论你努力想讲什么,他们很有可能都不感兴趣。

5. 作为人类,我们应该互相交流,让我们的世界和平安逸。

Situation Seven (Writing)

Situation：You have received an invitation to the wedding of your manager's daughter, you want to prepare a greeting card for the manager's daughter; at the same time, in order to make more friends on the wedding, you also want to have your own name card, so you are learning how to write them.

Task 1：Learn the samples and tips on greeting cards and name cards / calling cards / business cards.

贺卡(Greeting Cards)

贺卡的种类繁多,包括圣诞卡、生日卡等。礼卡与贺卡功能很相似,基本格式几乎一样。写贺卡和礼卡特别要注意以下几点。

(1)收卡人的姓名通常都出现在贺卡的左上角。表现形式很多。公务式贺卡通常采用 To...,Dear...,或者直接用名字称呼。

(2)赠卡人的姓名通常写在贺卡的右下角。出现形式也很多样。可以直接署赠卡人的名字,也可用赠卡人和收卡人之间关系的形式,如 your son。

(3)祝词一般置于贺卡中央,而且要讲究美观。

格式一：

To

　　　Best wishes for...

　　　　　　　　　　　　From

格式二：

Dear

　　　Best wishes to you...

　　　　　　　　　　　　Tom

格式三：

To

　　　Best wishes to you...

　　　　　　　　　　　　Your brother

Sample：

> To Mr. Zhang Yaoxian
>
> > Best wishes
> >
> > For
> >
> > Merry Christmas
> >
> > And
> >
> > Happy New Year
> >
> > > Yours sincerely,
> > >
> > > Li Guangyao

Useful Sentence Patterns

常用圣诞贺词

1. Merry Christmas!

   圣诞快乐!

2. May you have the best Christmas ever!

   祝你过一个最快乐的圣诞!

3. May the joy of Christmas be with you throughout the year!

   愿圣诞的快乐常年伴你。

4. May the blessings of Christmas be with you today and always!

   愿圣诞的祝福伴你今天,伴你永远!

常用新年贺词

1. Best wishes for the new year!

   把新年最好的祝福送给你!

2. I wish you a happy new year!

   祝你新年快乐!

3. Allow me to wish you a bright and prosperous new year.

   让我祝福你度过一个美好而又丰收的新年!

4. A happy new year to you and many of them!

   把千万个快乐的新年送给你!

母亲节贺词

1. Take good care of yourself. We all love you, Mom.

   好好保重自己。我们都爱你,妈妈。

2. You are the nicest mom in the world.

   你是世界上最好的母亲。

教师节贺词

1. You have been a great teacher and an even better friend.

　你一直都是一位伟大的老师,更是一位朋友。

2. I send you everlasting feelings of gratefulness and thankfulness.

　我把永远的感激和感谢送给你。

结婚贺词

Accept my sincere congratulations on your marriage with Mr. /Miss...

请接受我对你和……先生/女士婚姻的真诚的祝贺。

特殊成就贺词

1. Your years of hard work have paid off. Congratulations!

　祝贺你! 你多年的努力终于有回报了。

2. Please allow me to congratulate you most heartily on your success in your scientific research.

　请允许我为你在科学研究上取得的成就致以最衷心的祝贺。

3. I am very glad to hear of your great success...

　听说你取得了……成就,我很高兴。

4. I am very glad to hear that you have succeeded...

　很高兴听到你已经在……取得成功。

5. I am very delighted to hear that...

　很高兴听到……

6. I was greatly pleased to hear that...

　很高兴听到……

名片(Name Card / Calling Card / Business Card)

名片分为两种,即公务名片和私人名片。

公务名片格式如下。

正上方:供职单位名称

正中间:姓名及头衔或职称

左下方:地址及邮编

右下方:电话、电传及因特网址等

私人名片的格式如下。

正上方或正中间:姓名及头衔或职称

正中偏下方:供职单位名称及职务

左下方:地址及邮编

右下方:电话、电传及因特网址等

另外,英文地址通常是按照由小到大的顺序。如:Room 501, No. 28, Hongzhong Road，Shanghai，China.

Sample：

China International Import&Export Company

Wang Tianwang

General Manager

Address：No. 36 Lane 1122   Home Phone：(021)6459993

             Beijing Road Shanghai   Office Phone：(021)62450331

Zip Code：201104   E-mail：wang2005@sina. com. cn

Task 2：Writing practice.

1. 用所学的格式给你的朋友寄一张生日卡。

生日贺卡的内容：衷心祝您健康长寿。

2. 请为海河科技开发有限公司的周宝山副总经理译写一张名片。

地址：海河市和平区文化路三号巷 15 号

电话：3890760(办)、3914387(宅)

手机：13335478685

传真：(011)3890434

邮编：114709

Self-evaluation

Situation	Standard of Evaluation	Grade			Difficulties and Suggestions
		Excellent	Good	Improved	
Situation 1 Situation 5	I can talk about the item freely in a real situation.				
Situation 2-4	I can listen clearly and understand quickly.				
Situation 6	I can get the main idea of the passage in limited time, knowing about the importance of communication. I can translate the short passage well.				
Situation 7	I can write a practical greeting card and business card.				

Item Two   Food and Drink

Competence Objectives

1. Students can list some Chinese food and western food.
2. Students can know some differences between Chinese food and western food.
3. Students can know how to order food and drink in a restaurant.
4. Students can know something about fast food.
5. Students can write an invitation.
6. Students can write a reply to an invitation.

Warm-up Activities

Look at the following pictures and tell the names of the food. Which of them is your favorite? Speak out the reasons.

(   )   (   )   (   )   (   )

(   )   (   )   (   )   (   )

(   )   (   )   (   )   (   )

Situation One (Discussing)

Situation: Students are talking about their daily diet. They are discussing "what is a balanced diet". They tell each other what kind of food they have in their daily lives.

Task: Ask students to name as much food as possible in English and write them on the blackboard and group them. Teachers can ask the following questions.

1. What food do you like? Why?
2. What food do you dislike? Why not?
3. What food is good for us?
4. What food is bad for us?
5. What Chinese food do you know?
6. What western food do you know?

Situation Two (Listening)

Situation: It's a nice day. Jane and Hank meet at the school gate. It's been a long time since they saw each other last time. They are so excited that they want to plan something.

Task: Listen to the dialogue, and answer the questions according to the information you've heard. The conversation will be spoken twice.

1. What are they going to do?

2. What's the weather like?

3. When will they start?

4. Who will join them?

Situation Three (Listening)

Situation: Anita is good at cooking. Peter wants to cook something for his mother on her birthday party. So he turns to Anita.

Task: Listen to the dialogue, and answer the questions according to the information you've heard. The conversation will be spoken twice.

1. What kind of food does this dialogue mention?

2. What are its flavors?

3. Is it hard to make?

Situation Four (Listening)

Situation： Now western fast food is popular in China, and it becomes part of our lives. Do you know why?

Task：Listen to the record, and then tell the reasons. The passage will be spoken twice. Before you listen, learn the following words and expressions.

Words & Expressions	
tremendously　巨大地	efficient　效率高的
entertainment　娱乐	be related to　和……有关的
provide sb. with　向某人提供	benefit a lot from...　从……中获益

Situation Five (Speaking)

Situation： You and your friend go to a foreign restaurant for dinner.

Task：Make up a dialogue with your partner about how to order food and drink with the help of the following patterns.

1. May I have a menu, please?

2. May I order, please?

3. What is the specialty of the house?

4. Do you have today's special?

5. May I see the wine list?

6. May I order a glass of wine?

7. I'm on a diet.

8. How do you like your steak?

9. Could you recommend some good wine?

10. Well-done (medium/rare), please.

11. Could you tell me how to eat this?

12. Is coffee included in this meal?

13. Could you pass me the salt(pepper)?

14. I'd like a glass of water, please.

15. This is not what I ordered.

16. May I have some more bread, please?

17. I'd like a dessert, please.

18. We like to pay separately.

19. What do you have for dessert?

20. I think there is a mistake in the bill.

21. Can I pay with this credit card?

22. May I have the receipt, please?

Situation Six(◆ Speaking)

Situation: You and your friend are talking about the great changes of people's diet in China. Grain, which used to be the main food of most people in China, is now playing a less important role. People are fond of some western food. The changes in diet can be accounted for by a number of factors. What kind of reasons do you think might be?

Task:Now discuss the situation with your classmates, and then present your ideas before class. The following phrases and sentences will help you.

1. Higher income.

2. People have realized the importance of a balanced diet to their health.

3. Economic reform.

4. Insignificant as those changes may seem, they are the signs of the improved economic condition in China.

Situation Seven (　Reading)

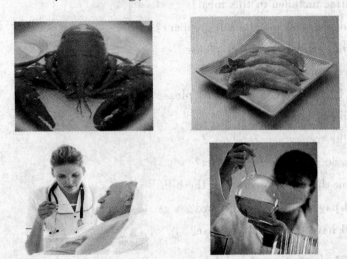

Situation：All the people want to know the relation between food and disease. Are all kinds of food good for our health? Can some of them cause disease? This passage will show you the recent research.

Task：**Read the passage to get the idea about what the research tells us and then finish the tasks.**

Food and Illness

The food we eat seems to have **profound**（极深的，深厚的）effects on our health. Although science has made enormous steps in making food more fit to eat, it has, at the same time, made many foods unfit to eat.

Some research has shown that perhaps eighty percent of all human illnesses are related to diet and forty percent of cancer is related to the diet as well, especially cancer of the **colon**（结肠，直肠）. Different cultures are some **prone**（易于……的，有……倾向的）to contract certain illnesses because of the food that is characteristic in these cultures.

That food is related to illness is not a new discovery. In 1945, government researchers realized that **nitrates**（硝酸盐）and **nitrites**（亚硝酸盐）, commonly used to preserve color in meats, and other food **additives**（添加剂）, caused cancer. Yet, these **carcinogenic**（致癌的）additives remain in our food, and it becomes more difficult all the time to know which things on the packaging labels of processed food are helpful or harmful.

The additives which we eat are not all so direct. Farmers often give **penicillin**（青霉素）to beef and poultry and because of this, penicillin has been found in the milk of treated cows. Sometimes similar drugs are administered (given) to animals not for medicinal purposes, but for financial reasons. The farmers are simply trying to fatten the animals in order to obtain a higher price on the market. Although the Food and Drug **Administration**（行政，行政机关）has tried **repeatedly**（重复地，再三地）to control these procedures, the practices continue.

Task 1：After reading the passage, decide which one is the best answer.

1. How has science done a disservice to mankind? _____ .

A. Because of science, disease caused by contaminated food has been virtually done away with

B. It has caused a lack of information, concerning the value of food

C. As a result of scientific intervention, some potentially harmful substances have been added to our food

D. The scientists have preserved the color of meats, but not of vegetables

2. What are nitrates used for? _____ .

A. They preserve flavor in packaged foods

B. They preserve the color of meats

C. They are the objects of research

D. They cause the animals to become fatter

3. What does FDA mean as an organization? _____ .

A. Food Direct Additives

B. Final Difficult Analysis

C. Food and Drug Administration

D. Federal Dairy Additives

4. The word carcinogenic means most nearly the same as _____ .

A. trouble-making

B. color-retaining

C. money-making

D. cancer-causing

5. Which of the following statements is not true? _____ .

A. Drugs are always given to animals for medical reasons

B. Some of the additives in our food are added to the food itself and some are given to the living animals

C. Researchers have known about the potential hazards of food additives for over thirty-five years

D. Food may cause forty percent of cancer in the world

Task 2: Choose one topic from the followings to discuss with your partner.

1. What do you know about the relation between food and illness?

2. Do you think food additives can cause cancer?

3. What kind of food do you think is healthy to our body?

Task 3: Translate the following sentences into English.

1. 科学在过去的五年里取得了巨大的进步。

2. 40%的癌症都和饮食有间接的关系。

3. 食品中的添加剂对人体是有害的。

4. 护士给她的胳膊注射了青霉素。

5. 农民们试图喂胖家禽，以求卖个更高的价钱。

Situation Eight (Writing)

Situation: Mr. Robert and Mrs. Robert are going to hold a party at their house. They want to invite some friends to attend it. So they decided to write invitations to their friends.

Task 1: After reading the following invitations, firstly you are expected to exchange your ideas about how to write an invitation and how to reply to it.

Informal Invitation

Dear Mr. White,

　　My wife and I would be very glad if you and your wife would come to dine with us next Saturday, the 26th, at 6:30P. M. , at the Hilton Restaurant. I will also invite a few other friends. We will have Karaoke at the Hilton Restaurant. I am sure you will like it.

Yours,
Robert

Formal Invitation

Mr. and Mrs. Smith Mailer request the
Pleasure of
Mr. and Mrs. Robert White's
Company at dinner at the Hilton Restaurant
On Saturday
May 26th, at six thirty P. M.

Task 2:Write a reply to the following invitation.

Informal Invitation

Dear John,

    Margaret and I would be happy to have you and Mary come and have dinner with us at our house at half past seven on Saturday evening.

Yours sincerely,

Harry

Self-evaluation

Situation	Standard of Evaluation	Grade			Difficulties and Suggestions
		Excellent	Good	Improved	
Situation 1 Situation 5-6	I can talk about the item freely in a real situation.				
Situation 2-4	I can listen clearly and understand quickly.				
Situation 7	I can get its gist in limited time. I can translate related sentences and the short passage well.				
Situation 8	I can write an invitation.				

Item Three   Tourism and Environment

Competence Objectives

1. Students can know different tourist attractions throughout the world.
2. Students can know how to describe one's likes and dislikes.
3. Students can know how to reserve tickets.
4. Students can know how to prepare for a trip.
5. Students can know the relation between tourism and environmental pollution.
6. Students can know how to choose summer season.
7. Students can write a complaint letter.

Warm-up Activities

Look through the following pictures, and try to find out where these famous landmarks are located? What words come to your mind when you look at each of these landmarks? Which one is the most beautiful? Why?

| Tower Bridge | Eiffel Tower | Statue of Liberty |

| Opera House | Pyramids | The Canals |

Taj Mahal   **The Great Wall**   **Warriors**

Situation One (Discussing)

Situation: With the approaching of National Day, Li Mei and her family plan to go out for a trip. However, it's a little bit difficult for them to decide where to go. Also the travel agency gives some recommendation by reading the following pictures. Have you ever been to the following tourist attractions? What are they?

Task 1:Say as much as you can about each of them.

Task 2: Discuss with your partner to know which place he or she wants to go to
and the reasons.

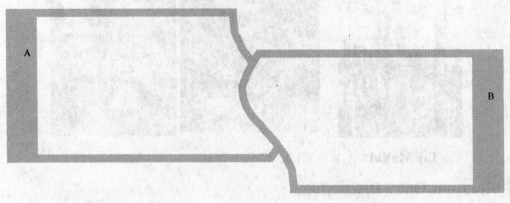

A

B

Situation Two (Listening)

Situation: Mr. Hanks is trying to reserve an air ticket.

Task: After listening to the dialogue twice, you are expected to tell others where
and how much should he pay.

1. Where does Mr. Hanks want to go?

2. How much should he pay?

3. When will the plan take off?

Situation Three (Listening)

Situation: Mark, an international student in Beijing, is fond of traveling around
China during vacation. Now he is talking about his latest journey
with his friend.

Task 1: Listen to the dialogue and decide whether the following statements are true
(T) or false(F).

1. Mark has just been back from a trip.

2. In summer, it is hotter in Wuhan than in Beijing because many people in
Wuhan like to use stoves.

3. Mark had enough time to go sightseeing when staying in Wuhan.

4. The food in Wuhan is not only delicious but cheap.

5. The Yellow Crane Tower is only place worth visiting in Wuhan.

6. Mark only got to the Yellow Crane Tower because it is the most famous tourist attraction.

Task 2: Listen to the dialogue again and then try to finish the following passage.

Mark has just been back from __1__ for __2__ . In his opinion, it is a __3__ city, in which the people are __4__ and the food is __5__ . But the weather there is so __6__ . There are many __7__ in Wuhan to go, but he only visited the most famous __8__ —The Yellow Crane Tower.

Situation Four (Listening)

Situation: Linda is a tourist guide, now she is introducing the scenic spot.

Task: Listen to the dialogue and choose the best answer to each of the questions you've heard.

1. Where is this tour taking place? _____ .

A. On the top of the mountain　　　　B. On the way up the mountain

C. Inside the mountain　　　　D. On the foot of the mountain

2. Which of the following does the tour guide NOT point out during the tour?

_____ .

A. Wild animals　　　　B. Scenery

C. Traditional sports　　　　D. Restaurant

3. What does the tour guide do after she points out Mirror Lake?

_____ .

A. She suggested all go swimming　　B. She introduced a little history of it

C. She quickly changed the topic　　D. She talked about the temperature

4. Which mountain is the highest according to the tour guide?

_____ .

A. Mount Lotus　　　　B. Mount Eagle

C. Mount Tianzhu　　　　C. The guide doesn't mention it

Situation Five (Speaking)

Situation: Suppose your mother will go out for a seven days' trip, you are asked to help her make preparations. What can you do?

Task 1: Discuss with your partner to know how to prepare for trip abroad, and then write them down.

Task 2 : **What are your favorite scenic spots in China? Write down the ones which impress you most and then make a short conversation with your partner. The following suggested sentence patterns will help you.**

1. Do you like traveling?

2. How many places have you visited in China?

3. What is the best time to go traveling?

4. What do you want to know?

5. I hear it is a good place for tourists.

6. It's really hot/cold.

7. It's really a beautiful city.

8. I enjoy my traveling very much.

Situation Six (　Speaking)

Situation : You have just been back from Beijing, and you find the Great Wall become dirty, as many visitors threw the rubbish and carved their names on the Great Wall.

Task 1 : **Look at the following pictures, discuss "Is it good for the whole nation to go out for a trip on National Day?"**

Task 2:What does tourism bring to your hometown?

Situation Seven (📻Reading)

Situation: Everyone likes traveling, but different people choose to travel in different seasons. Some prefer to travel in peak season, some maybe in non-peak season. How about the Americans?

Task:Read the passage to get the idea about traveling season for Americans and then finish the tasks.

Summer—Traveling Season

When asked which season is the best to travel, eight Americans in ten will answer "the summertime". Why? Because school is out. Because the weather is great. And most of all, because we all need a break. Once Americans take a break, they often head for their favorite vacation spot.

History **witnesses**(见证,证明) that Americans have been a nation on the move. The early **immigrants**(移民,侨民) had to travel to get to the New World. Once they arrived, they settled along the East Coast. But they weren't content to stay there. Explorers and traders journeyed to the unknown western **territories**(领土,版图;领地). Later, settlers moved west to develop these new areas. Even today, Americans seem unable to **stay put**(安装牢固,原位不动). Research says that the average American moves every five years.

Besides their habit of changing addresses, Americans are used to traveling. Some people take long-distance subways or trains to work daily. Their jobs may even require them to take frequent business trips. Most companies provide an **annual**(一年一次的,年度的)vacation for their employees, and people often use that time to travel. Some people just visit friends or relatives in distant states. Others go out for short-distance trip on weekends and stay in economy motels. Those with more expensive tastes choose **luxurious**（豪华的，奢侈的）**resorts**（常去的休闲度假之处；名胜）and hotels. Camping out in the great outdoors **appeals**（有吸引力，迎合爱好）to adventurous types.

Most Americans prefer to travel within their own nation. Why? For one thing, it's cheaper than traveling abroad, and there's no language problem. But besides that, the vast American territory offers **numerous**（许多的，很多的）tourist attractions. Major cities offer visitors a variety of urban delights. Nature lovers can enjoy beaches, mountains, **canyons**（峡谷）, lakes and a wealth of natural **wonders**（奇迹；奇观；奇事）. History **buffs**（迷，爱好者）seek out famous historical sites and museums. Some people find sea **cruises**（坐船旅行）relaxing and **refreshing**（使人耳目一新的，别有韵致的）. Others prefer to go fishing, skiing. The convenience of modern freeways, railways and airplanes makes travel in America as easy as pie.

Americans aren't the only people in the world who travel. International business, mass communication and **jet airplanes**（喷气式飞机）have made the world a global village. People all over the world enjoy going abroad to travel. And no matter where they live, people enjoy visiting scenic spots in their own country. But in America, almost everybody is a tourist sometime.

Task 1: Getting a message.

After reading the passage, decide whether the following statements are true (T) or false(F).

1. American prefers to travel in summer because they are on vacation at that time.

2. Through American history, Americans have been moving and changing their address.

3. In US, only the rich people have opportunities to go out for a trip and take annual vacation in spots.

4. Many Americans choose to travel at home simply because of the traveling cost.

5. Only Americans like traveling throughout the world.

Task 2: Skimming and scanning.

Scan the passage and answer the following questions.

1. Why do Americans prefer to travel in summer?

2. Why do Americans prefer to travel within their own nation?

3. What make traveling throughout the world as easy as a pie?

Task 3: Translate the sentences into English.

1. 他常到巴黎及别的地方去。

2. 她的幽默感把他强烈地吸引住了。

3. 一则我没钱，再则我也没有时间出去游玩。

4. 对国家著名历史古迹，应加以重点保护。

5. 我发现旅行的时候有必要搞到一张地图。

Situation Eight (✍ Writing)

Situation：You have just bought a computer from the Internet，but you found the machine damaged when receiving it. Now，you are writing a complaint letter to the company.

Sample：

Nov. 10，2003

Dear Manager，

I am writing to complain about the bad delivery service of your company.

The computer we ordered from your store two weeks ago finally arrived yesterday. There were not any signs of damage to the packing case at all，but when we opened it，we found，much to our surprise，that the back cover had been cracked and the screen had been scratched.

In view of this，I have decided to make a formal complaint against your delivery service. I sincerely hope that you will replace this computer as soon as possible. If this is impossible，I will have no alternative but to insist on a full refund.

Looking forward to your early reply.

Sincerely yours，

Jonathan Edwards

Task 1：After reading them，firstly you are expected to exchange your ideas about how to write a complaint letter with your partners，and understand the basic writing skills.

投诉信(Letter of Complaint)

在日常生活中，人们常会遇到对所购商品质量或售后服务不满意的情况，这时可以写投诉信求得解决。投诉信与普通书信的格式基本相同。一封正式的投诉信包含以下内容：题头(应写"投诉书")，其次是受理投诉的公司名称，如"××公司"，损害事实发生的过程以及交涉的情况，投诉请求和具体要求，被投诉方的单位名称、联系电话、地址、邮编等，投诉方的姓名、联系电话、地址、邮编等，投诉的日期和签名。

Useful Sentence Patterns

说明意图

1. I am writing to complain about. . . /that. . .

2. I am writing to express my dissatisfaction with somebody about something.

3. I am most reluctant to complain，but...

4. I feel sorry to trouble you but I am afraid I have to make a complaint about...

解释情况

1. When we checked... , we noticed...

2. When I took... out of the bag and examined... closely, I found...

3. When I unpacked... and tried to use it，it did not work.

解决方案

To solve the problem，I would appreciate it if you could repair.../exchange.../refund the money...

投诉信结尾

1. I would be grateful / I shall appreciate it very much if you could take the matter into consideration and solve it at your earliest convenience.

2. I would like to have this matter settled by the end of... / within 14 days.

Task 2：You have bought a brand-new computer in a store. But much to your disappointment, it could not be properly operated when you got it back. Write a letter to the manager.

1. Giving complaints.

2. Describing the problems.

3. Asking for some compensations.

Self-evaluation

Situation	Standard of Evaluation	Grade			Difficulties and Suggestions
		Excellent	Good	Improved	
Situation 1 Situation 5-6	I can talk about the item freely in a real situation.				
Situation 2-4	I can listen clearly and understand quickly.				
Situation 7	I can get its gist in limited time. I can translate related sentences and the short passage well.				
Situation 8	I can write a practical passage about the complaint letter.				

Item Four　Sports

Competence Objectives

1. Students can talk about sports freely in a real situation.
2. Students can know how to keep fit.
3. Students can know more about foreign culture and customs.
4. Students can write a practical passage about the poster and notice.
5. Students can know how to apply for a fitness card.

Warm-up Activities

After looking through the following pictures, please talk about your ways of sports.

Situation One (Discussing)

Situation: 2008 Olympic Games has been successfully held in Beijing. Many excellent athletes and Olympic events are still in our memories.

Task: Watch the pictures below and choose one to make dialogues with your partner. You may follow the model dialogue below.

A: Did you watch the performance of gymnastics last night?

B: Of course. I like it best. He Kexin won uneven bars, and her performance was too perfect!

A: Last night, her performance looked so relaxed and graceful.

B: She was quite an experienced gymnast! Not only the performance was perfect, but also the movements were quite to the music.

A: Right. She's a great gymnast.

田径 Athletics	马术 Equestrian	铁人三项 Triathlon	柔道 Judo	摔跤 Wrestling
足球 Football	篮球 Basketball	排球 Volleyball	沙滩排球 Beach Volleyball	乒乓球 Table Tennis

手球
Handball

曲棍球
Hockey

棒球
Baseball

射击
Shooting

体操
Artistic Gymnastics

羽毛球
Badminton

帆船
Sailing

水球
Water Polo

击剑
Fencing

蹦床
Trampoline

花样游泳
Synchronized Swimming

跆拳道
Taekwondo

自行车
Cycling

跳水
Diving

垒球
Softball

现代五项
Modern Pentathlon

皮划艇静水
Canoe/Kayak Flatwater

艺术体操
Rhythmic Gymnastics

拳击
Boxing

网球
Tennis

赛艇
Rowing

射箭
Archery

皮划艇激流回旋
Canoe/Kayak Slalom

游泳
Swimming

举重
Weightlifting

Situation Two (Listening)

Situation: John and Jerry both like sports. Now they are talking about it.

Task 1: Listen to the dialogue and decide whether the following statements are true (T) or false (F).

Words & Expressions	
ice-skating 滑冰	gymnasium 体育馆
influence 影响	

1. They are talking about a table tennis match.
2. Jerry often plays table tennis with his brother and sister.
3. They often go to the gym to play.

4. They will have a tennis table at home.

5. Jerry's parents are great lovers of table tennis.

Task 2: Listen to the dialogue again and change the italicized words with the words you hear from the dialogue.

1. What are you doing *besides* work?

2. I *liked* ice-skating, but now I *like* table tennis.

3. *Why* do you like table tennis?

4. My parents *like* it and they always say it's a great sport.

Situation Three (Listening)

Situation: As the old saying goes, where there's a will there's a way. To keep fit, one should keep doing exercise. Jeff and Sam are friends. Now they are talking about fitness.

Task 1: Listen to the dialogue and match Column A with Column B.

Words & Expressions	
fit　健康的	jog　慢跑
kid　开玩笑,取笑	couch　长沙发
couch potato　因长久坐在沙发上看电视不活动而发胖的人	

Column A	Column B
Jeff	1. lifts weights
	2. may start with some simple and easy exercise
	3. does bodybuilding
	4. is fit
	5. goes jogging
	6. exercises a lot
	7. seldom does exercise
Sam	8. watches TV
	9. gets up very early
	10. plays PC games

Task 2: Listen to the dialogue again and fill in the blanks with the information you've heard.

Sam: You're really fit. Do you _____ a lot?

Jeff：Yes, Sam. I always _____ very early, and _____ for an hour.

Sam：You're kidding!

Jeff：No, I'm _____ .

Sam：Wow! How often do you exercise like that?

Jeff：About four times a week. What about you?

Sam：Well, I seldom do exercise. I usually watch TV and play _____ in my free time.

Jeff：It's not surprising that we have so many _____ .

Sam：I really want to start to be fit. Do you have any _____ for me?

Jeff：Sure, if you can _____ .

Sam：I guess it's really hard for a beginner.

Jeff：You can start with some _____ exercise, like jogging or bicycling.

Situation Four (Listening)

Situation：Wimbledon Open（温布尔登网球公开赛）is the most important sporting event in Britain. It has a long history and has become a global sporting event attended by over half a million people.

Task：Listen to the dialogue and answer the following questions.

Words & Expressions

tournament　锦标赛,联赛	spectator　观众,旁观者
hallowed ground　圣地	monk　修道士
courtyard　院子,庭院	scoring　计分,得分
deuce　（还要继续比赛下去的）局末平分(2 平, 3 平, 4 平 ……)	
love　（网球）零分	

---

1. What has happened since the first tournament was played in 1877 in front of a few hundred spectators?

_____

2. How long is the history of the Wimbledon tennis championship?

_____

3. Which language is the origin of many words used in tennis?

_____

Situation Five (👄Speaking)

Situation: When you decide to take up a sport with friends, it's necessary to choose a good place and make some preparations.

Task: **Now make dialogues with your classmates about planning to do sports and report them in class.**

```
                      Expressions for Practice

Why don't we ...?                    How about...?
Shall we...?                          What if...?
Would you like to...?                 Let's...
```

Situation Six (👄Speaking)

Situation: Nowadays, more and more white-collar workers choose to do exercise in gymnasiums. Holding a fitness card is the best choice.

Task: **Make dialogues with your classmates about applying for a fitness card and report them in class.**

```
                      Expressions for Practice

How can I help you?                  What can I do for you?
What do you provide?                 I'm getting fat.
I'm a bit out of shape.              How much does it cost?
I'm thinking about exercising to keep fit.
How can I apply for a fitness card?
```

Situation Seven (👁Reading)

Situation: Sports are very common in each country. Here we learn American sports which have various forms. And sports make lots of sportsmen known around the world.

Task: **Read the passage to get the idea about sports in the US and then finish the tasks.**

Sports in the US

In many parts of the world, there are four seasons: spring, summer, fall and winter. In the US, there are only three: football, basketball and baseball. That's not **completely**(完全地) true, but almost. In every season, Americans have a ball. If you want to know what season it is, just look at what people are playing. For many Americans, sports do not just **occupy**(占据) the **sidelines** (旁线,侧道). They take center **court**(球场).

In addition to "the big three" sports, Americans play a variety of other sports. In warm weather, people enjoy water sports, such as **surfing**(冲浪), sailing and scuba **diving** (潜水)to the ocean. Swimmers and water skiers also **revel** (沉迷于) in the wet **stuff** (东西). Fishermen try their luck in **ponds**(池塘), lakes and rivers. In winter sportsmen **take delight in** (以……为乐) freezing fun. Frozen ponds and ice **rinks**(溜冰场)become playgrounds for skating and **hockey**(冰球). People play indoor sports in all weathers. **Racquetball**(壁球), **weightlifting**(举重) and **bowling**(保龄球) are year-round activities.

For many people in the US, sports are not just for fun. They're almost a **religion** (宗教). Thousands of sports fans buy expensive tickets to watch their favorite teams and athletes play. Other fans watch the games at home, **glued**(黏在……上) to their TV sets. The most **devoted**(挚爱的,忠诚的) sports **buffs**(爱好者) never miss a game. Many a wife becomes a "sports **widow**" (寡妇) during her husband's favorite season. America's devotion to athletics has **created**(创造)a new class of wealthy people—**professional**(职业的)athletes. Sports stars often receive million-dollar salaries. Some even make big money by **appearing**(出现) in advertisements for soft drinks, shoes and even **toiletries**(化妆品).

Americans make their sports and athletes known to the whole world. Satellites broadcast games to sports fans around the globe. **The World Series**(世界联赛) — the US professional **baseball championship**(棒球锦标赛), has begun to **live up to**(不辜负) its name. The names of American superstars like Air Michael Jordan have become **household**(家庭的) words over the world. Who knows? Sports seasons may even change world weather patterns.

Task 1: **Read the passage and you are required to read the questions and then complete the answers below them. You should write your answers as briefly as possible.**

1. By what can we judge the seasons in the US?

_____

2. How many water sports are mentioned in the passage? What are they?

_____

3. Where do people always skate and play hockey in winter?

_____

4. What are wives called when their husbands devote to sports?

_____

5. According to the passage, how do athletes make money in addition to sports?

_____

Task 2：Translate the sentences into English.

1. 那家店销售多种碟片。(a variety of)

2. 他特别喜欢乡村生活。(revel in)

3. 她老爱跟我打赌。(take delight in)

4. 他的脸紧贴在窗上。(be glued to)

5. 你必须实践自己的诺言。(live up to)

Situation Eight (✍ Writing)

Situation 1：A sports meeting is going to be held in your school. All students are invited to watch the competition. Here is a poster for the campaign.

POSTER

This Week's Sports Meeting

Time：8 A. M. —5 P. M. Saturday, April 10

Place：The playground

The School Students' Union

Situation 2：There're a lot of preparations for the sports meeting. All the gym teachers are required to discuss it. Here is a notice about the meeting.

NOTICE

August 14, 2008

All gym teachers are requested to meet in the conference room at 2：00 P. M. on Saturday, August 18.

Nanjin University

Task 1：Talk about the writing skills about poster and notice.

海报(Poster)

海报多是宣传广告。英文海报的内容常为球讯、影讯等,标题居中,发布单位写在右下角。

通知(Notice/Announcement)

通知是上级对下级、组织对成员或平行单位之间部署工作、传达事情或召开会议等所使用的应用文。通知要求言简意赅、措辞得当、时间及时。通知上方正中写 Notice 或 Announcement,发出通知的单位一般放在正文后右下角处,发出通知的日期写在右上角处。

Task 2: Write a poster and a notice according to the following directions.

1. The School Students' Union will play a free film named *Schindler's List* in the lecture hall at 6 P.M. on May 10. Follow the model above and write a notice.

2. 11 月 5 日,你以总经理办公室的名义起草一份通知,通知各董事会(director)成员参加年终董事会(board of directors)。通知内容如下:

(1)本年度最后一次董事会将于 12 月 1 日上午 10 点在会议室召开,请务必出席;

(2)会议提供午餐;

(3)如果无法出席,请于 11 月 15 日前电话通知。

MEETING NOTICE

_____

_____

_____

_____

Self-evaluation

Situation	Standard of Evaluation	Grade			Difficulties and Suggestions
		Excellent	Good	Improved	
Situation 1 Situation 5-6	I can talk about the item freely in a real situation.				
Situation 2-4	I can listen clearly and understand quickly.				
Situation 7	I can get its gist in limited time. I can translate related sentences and the short passage well.				
Situation 8	I can write a practical passage about the poster and notice.				

Item Five　Medical Care and Health

Competence Objectives

1. Students can know about some common health problems.

2. Students can know how to communicate with doctors and get help from the doctor.

3. Students can know how to own a healthy body.

4. Students can know some information about the medical insurance systems in different countries.

5. Students can know how to ask for a sick leave.

Warm-up Activities

After looking through the following pictures, please talk about what's the matter with them.

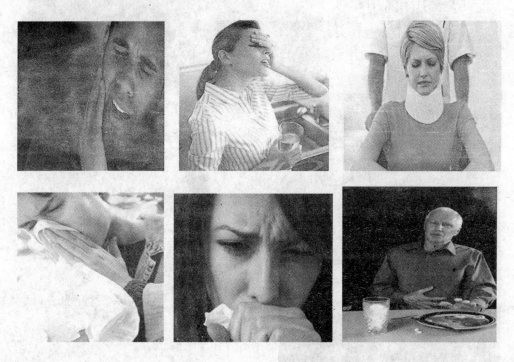

Situation One (Discussing)

Situation: You are talking about the health problem and discussing the following proverbs with your intimate friend.

Task: Do you know the meaning of the following proverbs? And how do you think of the health?

A. Sickness is felt, but health not at all.

B. Those who think they have no time for bodily exercise will sooner or later have to find time for illness.

C. Without healthy life is no life.

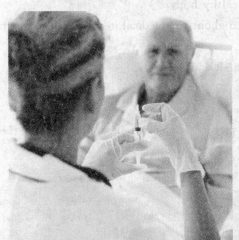

Reference

1. We all know that health is important, but many people do not pay much attention to their health unless they are ill.

2. I think that this is terribly wrong, because...

3. With good health, we can ...

4. Without good health, ...

Situation Two (Listening)

Situation: George has not felt well since yesterday, and he has a terrible headache now. In the morning, he comes to see a doctor in the hospital, and he answers the doctor's questions and gets a prescription and some advice.

Task: Listen to the dialogue and describe George's symptoms. Before listening, learn the following words and sentences which will help you.

Words & Expressions			
symptom	症状,征兆	blow up	爆炸
tuberculosis	肺结核	stuff up	塞住
influenza	流感		

Useful Sentence Patterns

1. Last night I suffered from insomnia(失眠).

2. I tried some sleeping pills，but they have done nothing for me.

3. I'm afraid I've got a temperature.

4. I've got a running nose.

5. I keep feeling dizzy.

6. I seem to have pain all over. / I'm aching all over.

7. I'm having some trouble sleeping.

8. I'm running a fever. /I'm running a temperature.

9. The trouble began yesterday.

10. I feel numb in my right arm.

11. I don't feel like eating anything.

12. I have been like this for about a week.

Situation Three (　Listening)

Situation：Nowadays，A/H1N1 flu has been almost spreading around the world and the number of infected people is increasing in some countries. You happen to see your friend Lily，who is a doctor.

**Task:Please listen to the dialogue and answer the following questions. Before lis-
tening, learn the following words and expressions.**

Words & Expressions	
contagious	传染性的,会蔓延的,会传播的
gauze	薄纱,纱布,金属网
virus	病毒
vaccine	疫苗
A/H1N1 flu	甲型 H1N1 流感

1. What are the two speakers talking about?

_____

2. What do you think of A/H1N1 flu according to the dialogue?

_____

3. What can we do to prevent A/H1N1 flu?

_____

Situation Four (Listening)

Situation: In addition to the daily maintenance of our bodies, water also plays a
key role in the prevention of diseases. Now listen to the following
passage and get more in depth about how much water we really need,
especially pay more attention to the quantity of water.

	Words & Expressions		
exaggerate	夸大,夸张	municipal	市政的,地方性的
contradict	同……抵触	filtration	过滤,筛选
pollutant	污染物	leaching	滤去

Task 1: Listen to the passage and fill in the blanks according to what you've heard.

We've heard for years that _____ glasses of water daily is the _____ necessary to keep healthy. Your weight loss and health _____ it. Drink the minimum and you will get clearer skin, better sleep, and _____ vision. But, the _____ has turned, away from liquid _____ toward examining your daily diet, including what you eat, as well as what you drink. The answer is that you need _____! If it's in summer, you need more. If you're doing exercise, you need more. If you're a "_____" person, always sit there, who's not sweeping, experts say that you need no more than four glasses of water daily.

Task 2: Answer the following questions according to the passage.

1. Why doesn't the author feel surprised that we are confused about how much water we should drink daily?

_____

2. How much water do we really need according to the author's explanation?

_____

3. How can we ensure the quantity and safety of the drinking water?

_____

Situation Five (◆Speaking)

Situation: Your friend Alice often can't go to sleep before a test or an exam, and she needs you to give her some suggestions to solve the problem.

Task: Now make up a dialogue with your partner to talk about the solution to the problem. The solutions for reference may help you.

1. Learn to accept the fact that exams and tests are part of students' life, so the best way is to learn to take them easy.

2. Failure in the exam doesn't mean the end of the world.

3. Find out the problems, overcome them and start again.

4. Exams and tests are just means to find out your strengths and weaknesses.

5. Do something else for a change.

Situation Six (☞ Reading)

Situation: Recently, medical insurance policy is drawing more and more attention of the public. Our government is focusing on the reform of the
medical system by benefiting some ideas from other countries' experience based on China's national condition. Therefore, it is necessary
for us to learn about some western countries' medical insurance poli-
cies.

**Task: Read the passage to get some information about the National Health Service
in the UK, and then finish the tasks.**

The National Health Service (NHS) provides health care in the UK and is
funded by taxation, which in general people don't have to pay for medical treatment. If you feel ill or worried about your health or the health of anyone of your
family, you should go to see the local doctor, called **General Practitioner**(GP)(全科
医生). The GP's clinic is called the Surgery or Health Centre. You should register
with a GP as soon as possible, so that you can get appropriate medical care if you
need it. To register you need to offer your name, date of birth, address and telephone number if you have one, which means that your name will be on the GP's
list, and you can make an appointment to see the doctor or call the doctor out to
visit you if you are ill. People sometimes do have to pay part of the cost of drug that
the doctor **prescribes**(开药方).

GPs are trained in general medicine but are not **specialists**(专科医生) in particular subject. If patients need to see a specialist doctor, they must first go to their
GP and then the GP will make an appointment with the patient before they see a
specialist at a hospital or a clinic.

Although everyone in the UK can have free treatment under the NHS, it is also possible for him to have treatment done privately, for which he has to pay. Some
people have private health insurance help them pay for the private treatment. Under
the NHS, people who need to go to hospital may have to wait for a long time according to a waiting list for their treatment. But anyone who is very ill also can call
an **ambulance**(救护车) and get taken to hospital for free urgent medical treatment. Ambulance is a free service in the UK.

Task 1: Getting a message.

Make your choice for the following exercises.

1. In the UK, the National Health Service refers to _____.

A. a local hospital

B. a medicine supplier

C. a medical care system

D. an insurance company

2. Under the National Health Service, the UK citizens _____ .

A. are all registered with a general practitioner

B. do not need to buy private health insurance

C. can only go to see a general practitioner

D. cannot call in a general practitioner

3. People buy private health insurance in order to _____ .

A. pay for the ambulance service

B. receive free urgent treatment

C. see a general practitioner

D. have private treatment

4. Which of the following is TRUE according to the passage?

A. People in the UK do not have to pay for any kind of medical care.

B. People in the UK may wait long for their free medical treatment.

C. In the UK you have to pay for ambulanceservice.

D. The UK private medical insurance is free.

Task 2:Skimming and scanning.

Answer the following questions after reading.

1. What is the source of funds about the National Health Service?

_____

2. How can you get medical care if you need in a GP's clinic?

_____

3. How does a patient see a specialist doctor?

_____

Task 3:Discuss the following topic with your partner.

As we all know, there are still some people, especially some migrant workers, who haven't bought medical insurance in China. Do you think it is necessary to buy medical insurance for every one? Why?

Situation Seven (✍ Writing)

Situation: Sophia has got a headache and a cough. She didn't sleep well last night and felt even worse this morning. Then she went to see a doctor. The doctor told her to have a good rest; otherwise it would get more serious. So she must ask for a sick leave. Please write a request for leave for her.

Task 1: Firstly you are expected to exchange your ideas about how to write a request for leave before reading the following reference.

请假条(Request for Leave)

(1)请假条往往指由于生病或特殊情况不能亲自当面请假,用假条的形式告假。所以,请假条大多是病假条。可以自己写,也可请他人代写。

(2)写请假条要注意把请假原因和请假时间写清楚,而且请假的理由要充分。如果有证明请假原因的证据,譬如医生证明或信件等,最好要随条附上。

(3)请假条书写格式可是书信或便条格式。

(4)请假条的特点要求开门见山、内容简短、用词通俗易懂。

Task 2: Write a request for a sick leave to her teacher according to the situation.

Dear Sir,

_____

_____

_____

_____

Self-evaluation

Situation	Standard of Evaluation	Grade			Difficulties and Suggestions
		Excellent	Good	Improved	
Situation 1 Situation 5	I can talk about the item freely in a real situation.				
Situation 2-4	I can listen clearly and understand quickly.				
Situation 6	I can get its gist in limited time. I can say something more about the related topic.				
Situation 7	I can write a practical passage about the request for leave.				

Item Six　Internet Life

Competence Objectives

1. Students can know different ways of communicating with other people.
2. Students can know advantages of the Internet.
3. Students can know how to chat online.
4. Students can know what IAD (Internet Addiction Disorder) is.
5. Students can know how to write an e-mail.

Warm-up Activities

How much do you know the Internet or WWW(World Wide Web)?

Situation One (Discussing)

Situation: With the fast development of the Internet, more and more people are accessing various online resources. You can exchange information with your friends freely online nowadays. Suppose you meet a friend near the Internet bar, and then you make a dialogue about the advantages of surfing the Internet with him.

Task: Make a dialogue with your friend and describe your opinions concerning surfing the Internet.

A: Do you think the Internet is good?

B: Of course! The Internet can help us learn more things. We can find information we need. And...

A: Wait, some people would agree with you. But I don't think so. Because more and more students become addicted to the Internet and they can't get rid of it, their grades get worse and worse rapidly.

B: But everyone needs relaxation. The students you mentioned just now feel relaxed a lot. So we can't draw the conclusion that the Internet is bad. It can help us in many ways. As students we can visit the school website and learn things we don't know before. Don't you think so?

A: Yeah. It's true. But there is much unhealthy information, too.

B: But there is still much useful information. Why do you only see the bad parts of the Internet?

A: Maybe you are right.

Surfing the Internet

More and more people like to surf the Internet now. Do you like to surf the Internet? I think you may say "Yes, of course". My answer is the same as yours. Surfing the Internet is one of the most important activities today. We can get plenty of information from the Internet. We can also learn on the Internet. Some people say that the world is smaller than before because of the Internet.

What is going on in other countries? How do people live in places far away? Is there a good sport game? What is life like in the deepest of the sea? If you want to know the answers to these questions, just turn on your computer and surf the Internet. You can know more and learn more about life, science and so on. Of course, there are many other ways of learning. But with the computer you can learn better and get more information easily. However, as a student, you should not spend too much time in surfing the Internet every day. Also, there is something bad on the Internet. Therefore, it is important for us to tell the good things from bad ones when we surf the Internet.

Situation Two (Listening)

Situation: My friends Li Hua and Zhang Tao are talking about the advantages of surfing the Internet.

Task: After listening to the dialogue twice, you are required to tell others what advantages the Internet has.

Words & Expressions	
trap	圈套,陷阱;设圈套,设陷阱
negative	否定的,负的,消极的;底片,负数;否定
impact	冲击,冲突,影响;挤入,撞击,对……发生影响

Advantages Mentioned in the Dialogue

There are so many _____ things there. Actually there are far more _____ impacts.

Simply by clicking some buttons, you can get information about all kinds of topics. _____ you are looking for, you will find it. Even if you want to have very _____ information, you will find it in a short time.

You can socialize with people. One could find more friends on the Internet than in _____. There are social communities on the Internet, like English Corners. One can go there to _____ his oral English.

Another big advantage of the Internet is the easy _____ information and it is very cheap. One can _____ songs, read novels, play games and so on. There are many web sites that offer _____ stuff.

Situation Three (Listening)

Situation: Do you like chatting online? What do you usually chat about with your friends online? In this section, someone will talk about his on-line chatting experience.

Task: After listening to the passage twice, you are expected to tell others the speaker's opinion.

Words & Expressions	
positive	肯定的,积极的,绝对的;正面的,正数的;阳性的
primarily	首先,主要地

Situation Four (Listening)

Situation: Li Da is reading an English article related to Internet Addiction Disorder. His friend, Li Shang is listening.

Task: After listening to the passage, please retell what you have heard.

Words & Expressions			
psychologist	心理学家	addiction	沉溺,上瘾
phenomenon	现象	satisfaction	满意
excessive	过多的,过分的		
significant	有意义的,意味深长的;重要的,重大的		

Situation Five (⟺Speaking)

Situation: Weekend is coming. Mike and Lily are making an appointment to surf the Internet.

Task: **Read the following dialogue first, and then imitate the speaking materials as follows.**

Mike: What are you up to this weekend?

Lily: I am going to surf the Internet for some information about Hainan Island.

Mike: I'm going to surf the net, too, to get some information about Chinese learning.

Lily: I can send you some websites that may be helpful to you.

Mike: Thanks. I need a virtual university website.

Lily: We can search on the net and I am sure we can find some.

Mike: Yes, and you can find some suitable virtual holiday destinations, too.

Lily: Nowadays the Internet has made people's lives more and more convenient.

Mike: Yes, even my parents do online shopping and chatting, and sometimes they play games online.

Lily: Even my little nephew can download cartoon movies by himself.

Situation Six (♫Reading)

Situation: One day Shang Xian was reading a piece of English coaching paper. An article related to online shopping in the paper drew his attention. We have selected its main part as follows.

Task: **Read the passage and finish the following tasks.**

Holiday Shopping Trends

The Internet is an exciting tool that not only puts vast information at your fingertips but also expands your shopping options like never before. Now, with only a few clicks of the mouse, you can go online to buy just about anything you need or want from airline tickets to rare antiques.

Shopping on the Internet can be economical, convenient, and no less safety than shopping in a store or by mail. Whether you're buying directly from a business or an individual, an online retailer or an Internet auction, shopping online can be fun, easy, practical, and economical. But, just as in the bricks and mortar world, the Internet shopping experience can be marred by unscrupulous dealers constantly devising new ways to deceive consumers out of their money.

The holiday shopping season has already begun, with 38% of survey respondents saying they started their holiday shopping in October. Long gone are the days that marked Thanksgiving weekend as the start of the holiday shopping season. An additional 22% will start shopping around November 1st. Women make up a larger percentage (48%) than men (31%) of those who have already started their shopping for the holidays.

An overwhelming 92% of the respondents expect to shop and buy more online this year than last year, showing the increased dependence on online shopping for the holidays. Almost half of respondents will do at least 50% of their shopping for the holidays online this year (47%), with 7% stating they would do all of their holiday shopping online.

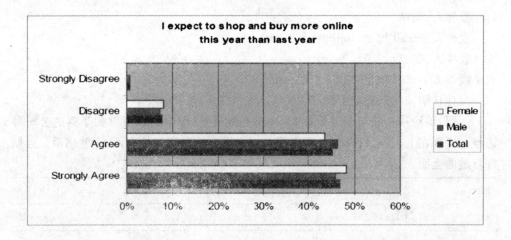

Task 1 : After reading the passage, decide whether the following statements are true(T) or false(F).

1. The Internet is an exciting tool that not only puts vast information at your fingertips but also expands your shopping options.

2. Shopping on the Internet can be economical, convenient, and no less safety.

3. Shopping online can be funny, difficult, practical, and economical.

4. Women make up a larger percentage than men of those who have already started their shopping for the holidays.

5. An overwhelming 92% of the respondents expect to shop and buy more online.

Task 2 : Choose one topic from the followings to talk with your partner.

1. What do you know about holiday shopping

2. What can you infer from the paragraph

Task 3：Translate the sentences into English.

1. 只要点击几下鼠标,你就能在网站上买到任何你想要的东西。

2. 网络购物经济、便利又安全。

3. 假期购物季节已经到来。

4. 在假日购物这个方面,女性占据了比男性更大的比例。

5. 我希望今年能比去年更多网络购物。

Situation Seven (✍ Writing)

Situation：This part is to test your ability to do practical writing. Han Mei is writing an e-mail to her former classmate Dai Li talking about network-based learning. First they are asked to read the following e-mail.

发件人：陆靖

发件人 e-mail 地址：lujing@163.com

收件人：李露

收件人 e-mail 地址：lilu@126.com

发件日期：2009 年 4 月 20 日

主题：预约——陆靖预定 5 月 20 日到上海出差,希望到时可以到李露的公司拜访她。计划在上海停留两周,希望李露可以安排合适时间与他会面,不胜感激。很期待与她的会面。

From：	lujing@ 163.com
To：	lilu @ 126.com
Subject：	Appointment in Advance
Date：	April 20th, 2009

Dear Li Lu,

    We haven't seen each other since we graduated from university in 2006. I am scheduled to visit Shanghai on business on April 20th, and wish to call on you at your office.

    I will stay in Shanghai for about two weeks. I would be very much appreciated if you'd like to arrange to meet me at your convenience.

    Thank you in advance for your kindness. I am looking forward to meeting you soon.

Sincerely yours,

Lu Jing

Task 1：You can exchange your ideas about how to write an e-mail with your predecessor before reading the following references.

电子邮件(E-mail)

E-mail 是现代社会常见的书信形式,一般是非正式的文体,其主要特点是简单明了,便于阅读。虽然电子邮件是非正式文体,但其撰写不可马虎,特别是给长辈、上级写信,或者撰写事务信函等。写完信后应仔细检查有无错误。书写电子邮件还要注意内容表达的清晰性和完整性。

Task 2: You are required to write an e-mail according to the following information.

发件人:韩梅

发件人 e-mail 地址:hanmei012@163.com

收件人:戴丽

收件人 e-mail 地址:daili-rose@126.com

发件日期:2009 年 4 月 20 日

主题:网络化学习——无须在校学习就可以磨炼强化职业技能,网络化的在线学习网站成千上万。几十年来,很多学生转向包括函授学习方式的远程学习来强化自身教育。远程学习满足了那些没有时间进课堂的人的需要。随着网络技术的快速发展,人们可以利用电脑进行虚拟课堂的学习。所需的只是电脑、浏览器与登录网络。

Words & Expressions

hone	磨炼,用磨刀石磨
mushroom	迅速生长,迅速增加
decade	十年
correspondence	相应;通信,信件
explosion	爆发,扩张
browser	浏览器;吃嫩叶的动物;浏览书本的人

From:	
To:	
Subject:	Network-based Learning
Date:	

Dear Dai Li,

Sincerely yours,

Han Mei

Self-evaluation

Situation	Standard of Evaluation	Grade			Difficulties and Suggestions
		Excellent	Good	Improved	
Situation 1 Situation 5	I can talk about the item freely in a real situation.				
Situation 2-4	I can listen clearly and understand quickly.				
Situation 6	I can get its gist in limited time. I can translate related sentences and the short passage well.				
Situation 7	I can write a practical passage about an e-mail.				

Item Seven   Lifelong Education

Competence Objectives

1. Students can learn about what lifelong education is and why we should keep on learning.

2. Students can talk about the education systems in major developed countries.

3. Students can learn the similarities and differences, advantages and disadvantages between China and other western countries.

4. Students can write a practical passage about sports posters.

Warm-up Activities

Look at the following pictures and talk about education according to your comprehension.

Situation One (Discussing)

Situation: When talking about "Lifelong Education", different people have different views on it. Some people simply think education is going to schools or colleges. The aim of education is also defined as a means to secure good jobs. But most people just have an opposite opinion. They consider education as a lifelong process, not only in childhood and youth. They believe that it is never too old to learn. As long as you want to learn, it is never too late to start. As far as I'm concerned, I agree with most people's attitude. I'm studying in a college and receiving good education now. But it doesn't mean that my education will come to the end with a college diploma in hand. Many things are awaiting for me to learn and to discover. I will make learning as my lifelong pursuit.

Task: **According to the above ideas, discuss the following two questions.**

1. What does "Lifelong Education" mean to you?
2. Is education for getting a good job or for improving yourself?

Situation Two (Listening)

Situation: Diane and Ken are talking about the evening class.

Task: **Listen to the following dialogue and then tell your partner why Ken took part in the evening class.**

Situation Three (Listening)

Situation: There is a dialogue between Mike and Diana, who are classmates. They are talking about choosing courses.

Task: **Listen to the dialogue and then answer the two questions below.**

1. What kind of lecture is Mike going to study this afternoon?
2. Why does Mike think the business communication course is difficult?

Situation Four (Listening)

Situation: Most students have no idea about the future educational forms and learning styles. The discussion will give us some information about new changes in education.

Task: **Listen to the passage below and decide whether the following statements are true (T) or false (F).**

1. The lecture introduces new educational forms and learning styles.

2. Future classrooms will be full of computers.

3. Students will have to take more courses in the future.

4. In future, students may take courses he or she likes in different universities.

5. Students in the future still have to pass the exams before entering university.

6. Students in the future will pay more tuition for their higher education.

Situation Five (👄Speaking)

Situation: Two college seniors are discussing their future plans for further education after graduation.

Role A: You're planning to continue your education as a graduate student, thinking that the more education you get, the more chances you will have to find a better job with a higher salary.

Role B: You've decided to find a job first and then join some training programs while working, believing that experience and practical skills are more important than knowledge from books.

Task: Work with a peer and take turns to start the conversation. The following may help you.

1. ... be better equipped before plunging into the society.

2. ...expect a better job with a higher degree.

3. It's a waste of time.

4. Work experience and practical skills are more valuable.

5. Master's degree, certificate, practice, promotion, interview, first-hand experience, flexibity, training class, on-line study ...

Situation Six (👄Speaking)

Situation: Two students are talking about their parents getting involved in continuing education programs.

Role A: Your mother has devoted most of her life to you and your family. Now she wants to go on studying to pursue the dream she ever had when she was young—to be a fashion designer. You strongly support her decision.

Role B: You don't think it's necessary for the elderly to take the trouble. They should relax and enjoy lives since they have spent most of their lives working and taking care of their children.

Task: **Work with a peer and take turns to start the conversation. The following**
will help you.

1. One is never too old to learn.

2. ... to use 99% rather than 60% of one's potential.

3. She doesn't want to die for doing only this!

4. I'm definitely for continuing education.

5. Count me out.

6. Retirement, relaxation, leisure, peace and quiet, carefree, pension, social
welfare...

7. ... accompanied by children and grandchildren.

Situation Seven (Reading)

Situation: Everyone has his own ideas about lifelong education. They are inquiring an expert to give them some ideas for their future education.

Task: **Read the passage and complete the following tasks.**

Be Realistic, College Students

Some students believe that once they have college degrees the world will be
waiting **on their doorsteps**(在门口), ready to give them wonderful jobs. But the reality is that unless they are planned, there will be nobody on their doorsteps.

I still remember the way our teacher **dramatized**(使戏剧化) this point in our
first class. He played as a student who had just obtained a college degree. He
opened up an **imaginary**(想象的) door, stepped through it, and looked around in
both directions outside. There was nobody to be seen. I understood the point he
made immediately: A college degree isn't enough. We have to get prepared for future while we are in college to make sure our degree is a **marketable**(有市场价值的)
one.

From then on, I began to think seriously about what I wanted to do in future
and whether there were jobs that I wanted. I went to the counseling center and
said, "I want to learn where the best job opportunities will be in the next ten
years." The **counselor**(顾问) referred me to a copy of the *Occupational*(职业的)
Outlook published by the United States government. The book has good information on what kind of jobs are available now and which career field will need workers
in the future. In the front of the book is a helpful section on job hunting.

The result of my personal career planning was that I graduated from Atlantic
Community College with a degree in **accounting**(会计,会计学). Then I got a job almost immediately, for I had chosen an excellent employment area. The firm that I

worked for paying my **tuition**(学费) as I went on to get my bachelor's degree. They're now paying for my work toward **certification**(证书) as a CPA (Certified Public Accountant), and my salary increases regularly.

I'm not saying that college should serve only as a training ground for a job. People should take some courses just **for the sake of**(为了……的利益) learning and for expanding their minds in different directions. At the same time, unless they have an **infinite**(无限的) amount of money, at some point, they must be ready to take **career-oriented**(以就业为目标的) courses so that they can survive in the changing world outside.

Task 1: Skim the passage and check your understanding by making the correct choice.

In the author's opinion, a college student should take _____.

A. no courses designed to open their minds

B. no courses for the sake of learning

C. job-related training courses only

D. both knowledge-based and job-oriented courses

Task 2: Choose the proper word or phrase in the box to fill in the blank in each of the following sentences, making changes if necessary.

in one's case	on one's doorsteps	make a point	in itself	make sure
refer to	for the sake of	as it is	available	expand

1. When he comes across new words in his reading, he often _____ a dictionary.

2. _____, it is Johnson who designed this homepage.

3. A lot of firms are taking this advantage to _____ their business.

4. Fresh vegetables are not in season now, but you can still find various vegetables _____ on the market.

5. The writer did his utmost to use simple language _____ easy comprehension.

6. Generally a doctor will spend ten years studying before he can be out in practice. But _____, his studies only lasted eight years.

7. We all understand that he is trying to _____, but we simply can't figure it out.

8. The little girl dreamt of a fairy lady standing _____.

9. His suggestion _____ is practicable. But we should think more

about how to make use of it.

10. You must _____ that everyone gets the message.

Task 3: Translate the sentences into English.

1. 很有可能他们弄错了密码(password)，所以我们无法登录(log into)进入这个网站。

2. 1990 年，她从广州外贸大学毕业，获得了经济学学士学位。

3. 我并非说享受人生不好，但是在人生的某个阶段我们总得要奋斗吧。

4. 你必须不断地学习来扩大自己的视野，只有这样你才能在富有挑战性的社会立足。

5. 除非他能马上改掉说谎的坏毛病，否则他就得永远不断地找工作。

Situation Eight (✍ Writing)

Situation: You and your friends are skimming through some posters on campus and are interested in some sports posters.

Sample 1

Exciting Women's Volleyball

Liaoning Women's Volleyball Team is to challenge the PLA Women's Volleyball Team in our city! Both teams are very powerful and have first-rate players! CCTV Sports Channel will have live broadcast!

Time: 1:30 P. M. , Jan. 3 (Tuesday)

Place: The Olympic Stadium

Sample 2

Rowing Game for the Dragon Boat Festival

This is a friendly game among the 9 departments of our college

both as an event of the university Spring Sports Games,

and to mark the Chinese Dragon Boat Festival.

Please come to cheer for the rowers and

enjoy the spring sunshine!

Time: 3:30 P. M. , May 5, 2010

Place: The Fascinating East Lake

Task 1：**After reading them, your friends talk about their ideas about how to write a sports poster and understand his basic writing skills.**

Useful Phrases

aquatic sports　水上运动

champion and runner-up　冠亚军

cross-country　越野

discus throw　掷铁饼

equestrian sports　马术

exchange sides　交换场地

finish line 终点线

football league　足球联赛

4×100m relay　四乘一百米接力

foul play　犯规

goal keeper　守门员

gymnastic sports　体操运动

half time　半场

high jump　跳高

International Olympic Committee　国际奥委会

opening ceremony　开幕式

the Olympic motto　奥运会座右铭

the Olympic flame　奥运会火炬

Task 2：**Translate the following poster into English, referring to the samples and the Data Bank for reference.**

精彩激烈的国际足球比赛赛讯

中国队 对 德国队

地点：首都体育馆

时间：2010 年 4 月 28 日下午三点半

请到接待处购票，欢迎前往助兴！

Self-evaluation

Situation	Standard of Evaluation	Grade			Difficulties and Suggestions
		Excellent	Good	Improved	
Situation 1 Situation 5-6	I can talk about the item freely in a real situation.				
Situation 2-4	I can listen clearly and understand quickly.				
Situation 7	I can get its gist in limited time. I can translate related sentences and the short passage well.				
Situation 8	I can write a practical passage on a sports poster.				

Item Eight   Advertising

Competence Objectives

1. Students are required to figure out the features of advertising slogans.
2. Students are required to discuss pros and cons of commercial advertisements.
3. Students are required to discuss tricks of bait-and-switch for advertising.
4. Students are required to discuss the celebrity advertising.
5. Students are required to understand what advertising is.
6. Students are required to write an ad with the offered information.

Warm-up Activities

Advertising is a form of communication used to influence individuals to purchase products or services or support political candidates or ideas. Frequently it communicates a message that includes the name of the product or service and how that product or service could potentially benefit the consumer. We are having too much advertising. Ads seem to be everywhere. Now read the following dialogues, and discuss the features of advertising slogans.

Dialogue 1
A: I'm thirsty. I want some coke.
B: Good. "Obey your thirst."
A: Ah. "The taste is great."
B: "I'm loving it!" Why not "ask for more"?

Dialogue 2
A: I personally like the slogan of Ricoh photocopier: "We lead. Others copy."
B: Me, too. It is short and sweet. I especially like the double intender(双关语) "copy". It's so witty.
A: I also like Maxwell's slogan: "Good to the last drop." There's such a feeling of warmth.
B: But Nestlé's seems to catch on. "The taste is great!" may appear closer to life. We can say it every day whenever we like what we are eating.
A: I guess good slogans should be catchy.

Situation One (Discussing)

Situation: Advertising slogans are short, often memorable phrases used in advertising campaigns. They are claimed to be the most effective means of drawing attention to one or more aspects of a product. Everyone is exposed to advertising slogans of all kinds. An effective slogan usually:

(1) states the main benefits of the product or brand for the potential user or buyer;

(2) implies a distinction between it and other firms' products—of course, within the usual legal constraints;

(3) makes a simple, direct, concise(简练的), crisp(新奇的), and apt (恰当的) statement;

(4) is often witty(言辞诙谐的);

(5) adopts a distinct "personality" of its own;

(6) gives a credible impression of a brand or product;

(7) makes the consumer feel "good";

(8) makes the consumer feel a desire or need;

(9) is hard to forget—it adheres to one's memory (whether one likes it or not), especially if it is accompanied by mnemonic(助记的) devices, such as jingles(短歌), ditties(歌谣), pictures or film.

Task 1: Read the following advertising slogans, and discuss which one impresses you most. Speak out your reasons.

1. World in hand, Soul in Cyber.

2. Good to the last drop.

3. Time is what you make of it.

4. A fair skin now, Dabao knows how.

5. Connecting people.

6. We lead. Others copy.

7. The relentless pursuit of perfection.

8. A diamond lasts forever.

9. Newton was wrong.

10. Apple thinks different.

11. Mosquito Bye Bye Bye.

12. Start ahead.

Task 2：Look at the following pictures, and match them with their advertising slogans given in Task 1.

(   )   (   )   (   )

(   )   (   )   (   )

(   )   (   )   (   )

( )

( )

( )

Situation Two (Listening)

Situation: Nearly all TV programs are accompanied with ads, which take up almost half of the show time. Grace and Andy are watching TV. Ads appear time and time again, and Grace gets annoyed. Here is their conversation.

Task:Listen to the dialogue, and choose the best answer to each of the questions you've heard.

1. According to Grace, what percentage of TV commercials is annoying?

A. 9%   B. 19%   C. 90%   D. Not mentioned

2. How often do TV commercials appear during a episode?

A. every 5 minutes   B. every 15 minutes

C. every 25 minutes   D. every 30 minutes

3. Which of the following statements about advertising are NOT mentioned in the dialogue?

A. boring   B. entertaining

C. smart   D. stupid

4. Where does the dialogue take place?

A. in the bathroom   B. in the dormitory

C. in the living room   D. in the dining room

5. What attitude towards ads does Andy hold?

A. positive   B. negative

C. neutral(中立的)   D. vague(模棱两可的)

Situation Three (Listening)

Situation: Manufacturers spend huge sums to enlarge their market share, and they will present the well-known people to praise their products. Andy's cousin, Mark, who worships the football star Beckham, is visiting Andy, and finds Andy has the same jacket advertised by Beckham. Here is their conversation.

Words & Expressions			
jealous	妒忌的；吃醋的	credibility	可信性，确实性
celebrity	名人，名流；名声，著名		

Task: **Listen to the dialogue, and answer the following questions.**

1. Why does Andy say Beckham would have bigger pockets to hold all the money paid for the ad?

_____

2. Is Andy jealous? Why or why not? Speak out your reason.

_____

3. Why do many companies often name celebrities as their spokesperson?

_____

4. Do celebrity ads always work? Why or why not? Speak out your reason.

_____

Situation Four (Listening)

Situation: Companies often name celebs as their spokesperson, and they believe celebrity effect can bring them fame and popularity. Some people tend to buy celeb advertised products. Grace, who is something of an actress, is invited to endorse a perfume(代言香水). She hesitates, and is concerned whether the brand depicts her perfectly or not. Therefore, Andy helps her find information about endorsements in advertising. Here is a passage Andy finds out, of which some words are missing.

Words & Expressions	
assign	分配,分派;派定,指定,选派
depict	描画,雕出;描述,描写
thorough	彻底的,完全的;十分仔细的
charity	博爱,慈善,施舍;善举;慈善团体
utilize	利用
endorsement	背书;赞同,支持;宣传
project	计划,规划;投射(光线等),投映
identity	身份,本体;同一
sustain	支撑,承受;维持,供养;忍受,禁得起
conflict	矛盾,冲突,斗争
bald	秃顶的;无草木的;赤裸裸的;无装饰的,单调的

Task: **Listen to the passage, and you are required to fill in the missing words according to what you have heard. The passage will be read twice.**

Celebrities are people who enjoy public recognition by a large number of people. ___1___ is hugely influenced by famous people. Marketing experts analyzes ___2___ of the celebrities to properly assign them to the brand which depicts them perfectly. Their ___3___ are reviewed thoroughly to assign them ___4___ .

Today, ___5___ of the advertising industry utilizes celebrity endorsement. A celebrity is bound to endorse many products and brands over a course of time. Each time a different image of the celebrity is being projected to the public. The company should keep in mind ___6___ and play accordingly. Projecting a different person every time will ___7___ , but at the same time the two identities shouldn't ___8___ . The captain of England soccer team David Beckham has endorsed many products. While advertising for Gillette, ___9___ was considered and he was given ___10___ .

Situation Five (≪≫Speaking)

Situation: The advertisements are everywhere, and they stick in our minds. Grace and Andy are talking about pros and cons of advertising. Here is their conversation.

Grace: We are having too much advertising. Ads are everywhere.

Andy: But to me advertising is informative. It helps me find out about new products.

Grace: New but may not be needed. That's how they grab customers like you.

Andy: Advertising can help me compare things I want to buy. It saves me a lot more time than trying to find out about things myself.

Grace: Come on, ads only influence your choice. They only tell you how good the products are.

Andy: That's fine so long as they don't tell lies.

Grace: Aren't we having enough false ads? They are capable of talking you into trying their amazing products.

Andy: I only trust big companies. Anyway, whether you like it or not, advertising won't go away.

Words & Expressions	
informative	情报的;见闻广博的;教育性的,有益的
grab	攫取,抓取;夺取,霸占;将……吸引住,影响

Task 1: Read the dialogue, and discuss what ads can bring us.

Pros: _____

_____

_____

Cons: _____

_____

_____

Task 2: Imitate the dialogue, and make a new one with the following useful sentences.

1. Ads produce the positive image of a product.
2. Ads make the products attractive.
3. Ads create consumer brand loyalty.
4. Advertising helps companies introduce new products.
5. Advertising helps companies sell more products.
6. Too much advertising confuses customers.
7. Pop-up(弹起的)advertising is disturbing.
8. Ads are misleading sometimes.
9. Ads make a hype(天花乱坠的广告宣传)about goods.
10. Whether you like or not, there will be even more advertising.
11. Whether you like or not, advertising won't get any less.

Situation Six (◇Speaking)

Situation: Some ads mislead us by playing the tricks of bait-and-switch(诱售
法). Grace is complaining to Andy about misleading ads. Here is
their conversation.

Grace: I find that quite often we buy something because the ad says it's good.

Andy: It may be good, but manufacturers spend a load of money advertising,
then we're going to be paying more for it if we buy their products.

Grace: That's true. The cost of the ads is built into the products.

Andy: Otherwise how could they get back the huge sums they put into advertising.

Grace: You were saying. I thought the jeans were 60% off, but actually I
bought them at 30% off.

Andy: Some ads mislead us by using small print.

Grace: Exactly. I later noticed that the ad read "Up to 60% off". But they used
very small print for "up to".

Andy: Next time remember to keep an eye out for hidden information.

Task 1: Read the dialogue, and discuss with your partner the following questions.

1. Why have we often been persuaded to buy something?

2. Why do we need to pay more for the products?

3. Why did Grace buy the jeans only at 30% off?

Task 2: Practice in groups and act out the dialogue.

Situation Seven (♪Reading)

Situation: Celebrity endorsement advertising is a prevailing advertising technique. More and more marketers choose to utilize multiple celebrities to promote their products or brands. With the help of Grace and
Andy, Alice learns more about advertising. Finally, she accepts the
invitation and endorses the perfume. Through advertising, Grace is
aware of what advertising is. Here is her understanding.

Advertising

Advertising is defined in Webster's dictionary as "the act or practice of calling people's attention to one's product, service, need, etc. , especially by paid announcements in newspaper and magazine, over radio or television, on **billboard** (广告牌), etc. "

Advertising is a form of communication used to influence individuals to purchase products or services or support political candidates or ideas. Frequently it communicates a message that includes the name of the product or service and how that product or service could potentially benefit the consumer. Advertising often attempts to persuade potential customers to purchase or to consume a particular brand of product or service. Modern advertising developed with the rise of mass production in the late 19th and early 20th centuries.

Commercial advertisers often seek to generate increased consumption of their products or services through branding, which involves the repetition of an image or product name in an effort to associate related qualities with the brand in the minds of consumers. Different types of media can be used to deliver these messages, including traditional media such as newspapers, magazines, television, radio, billboards or direct mail. Advertising may be placed by an advertising agency on behalf of a company or other organization.

Organizations that spend money on advertising promote items other than a consumer product or service include political parties, interest groups, religious organizations and governmental agencies. Non-profit organizations may rely on free modes of persuasion, such as a public service announcement.

Money spent on advertising has increased in recent years. In 2007, spending on advertising was estimated at more than $150 billion in the United States and $385 billion worldwide, and the latter to exceed $450 billion by 2010.

Task 1: Read the passage, and put the following statements in the correct order according to the reading.

A. Money spent on advertising has increased in recent years.

B. Advertising can influence individuals to purchase products or services.

C. Advertising is the act of calling people's attention to one's product, service, need, etc.

D. Organizations such as governmental agencies will spend money on advertising.

E. Advertising may be placed by an advertising agency on behalf of a company or other organization.

F. Different types of media can be used to deliver these messages.

1. _____ 2. _____ 3. _____ 4. _____ 5. _____ 6. _____

Task 2: Read the passage again, and find the supporting details for the following ideas of the passage.

Ideas	Details
Advertising is a form of communication.	
Media used to deliver advertising messages.	
Organizations that spend money on advertising.	
Money spent on advertising in recent years.	

Task 3: Translate the following sentences into Chinese.

1. Advertising is a form of communication used to influence individuals to purchase products or services or support political candidates or ideas.

_____

2. Advertising communicates a message that includes the name of the product or service.

_____

3. Advertising often attempts to persuade potential customers to purchase or to consume a particular brand of product or service.

_____

4. Modern advertising developed with the rise of mass production in the late 19th and early 20th centuries.

_____

5. Commercial advertisers often seek to generate increased consumption of their products or services.

_____

Situation Eight (⬌ Writing)

Situation: The use of celebrity endorsers(明星代言)in advertising is widespread—as much as 20 percent of all advertising use celebrity endorsers. Grace's endorsement has proven to be successful, and she accepts more endorsements. Here are the ads.

The first truly feminine cigarette—almost as pretty as you are. Women have been feminine since Eve, now cigarettes are feminine. Eve, also with menthol.

You'll wonder where the yellow went. When you brush your teeth with Pepsodent.

It beats as it sweeps as it cleans.

Aren't you glad you use Dial? Don't you wish everybody did?

When Cathy Cole and Peggy Burton saw Joan Emery's new floor, they couldn't believe their feet.

Vacation is a world where there are no locks on the doors or the mind or the body.

Task 1: Read the ads, and discuss with your partner how to write an ad.

Task 2: Write an ad for GEMBA Jewelry.

GEMBA 为首饰运营商,其品牌定位为"知性、简约"。GEMBA 广告语要求如下:

(1)广告语富哲理性,且意境深远;

(2)语言感染力强,且具时代性;

(3)文字规范,言简意赅,控制在 12 词以内。

Self-evaluation

Situation	Standard of Evaluation	Grade			Difficulties and Suggestions
		Excellent	Good	Improved	
Situation 1 Situation 5-6	I can talk about the item freely in a real situation.				
Situation 2-4	I can listen clearly and understand quickly.				
Situation 7	I can get its gist in limited time. I can translate related sentences.				
Situation 8	I can write an ad according to given information.				

Item Nine   Hotel

Competence Objectives

1. Students can get familiar with some facilities offered by a hotel.

2. Students can know how to reserve a hotel and how to respond to a hotel reservation.

3. Students can know how to check in a hotel and how to serve a guest in the reception desk.

4. Students can know how to check out a hotel and know how to deal with customers' problems as a waiter.

5. Students can learn to identify who should shoulder the responsibility in a certain situation.

6. Students can figure out the history of a hotel.

7. Students can know how to order and respond to a guest's order.

8. Students can fill in the form of registration and questionnaire in English.

Warm-up Activities

Have you got the experience of staying in a hotel? What are the decisive elements for you to choose a certain hotel?

Situation One (Discussing)

Situation: A relative of your family will come to your house next week. You haven't met for years, so you want to reserve a hotel to entertain him.

Task1: Discuss the following things with your parents.

1. Decide the kind of hotel you want and understand the food rates.
2. Decide the species of food.
3. Decide the specific time for the dinner.

**Task 2:You make a phone call to a restaurant to make a reservation for the meal,
and ask your partner to play the role of the operator in the reception
desk.**

Useful Sentence Patterns

1. I'd like to make a reservation.

2. What is it going to be, Chinese food or Western food?

3. How many are you?

4. Anything special on the menu?

5. What time would you like to come?

6. We're already booked out for eight o'clock, but we can fit you in at eight-thirty.

7. Okay, we look forward to seeing you.

8. We are all booked up at that time.

9. Smoking section or non-smoking section.

Situation Two (🔊Listening)

**Situation:Tom and Mary are newly married couple. They want to have a honeymoon in Hawaii. But they do not have much money, so they have
to budget well.**

Task 1:Pre-listening questions.

Finding a cheap hotel is important to budget travelers, whether for a Hawaiian
honeymoon, adventure travel, or for business.

1. How do you find a budget hotel: online through a hotel reservation website, in a guidebook, or in the phone book?

2. What questions would you ask if you called to make a hotel reservation?

Task 2:Listen to the dialogue and fill in the blanks.

Words & Expressions	
available	可用的,可得到的,有用的,有效的
kitchenette	小厨房
sauna	桑拿浴,蒸汽浴
suite	随员,套房,一组

1. For which day does the man make a reservation finally?

2. What kind of room does the man prefer?

3. Why doesn't he want to reserve the suite?

4. Including tax, how much is the man's room?

5. How do you spell the man's last name?

Situation Three (Listening)

Situation: Janet and Peter used to be schoolmates. Two years ago they graduated from college and haven't seen each other since then. They
bump into each other at today's business party.

Task 1: Pre-listening discussion.

Discuss with your partner about the types of room in a hotel and what kind of
room you'd like to choose when you check in a hotel.

**Task 2: Listen to the dialogue between the guest and receptionist and find the an-
swers to the following questions.**

Words & Expressions		
check in	登记	

1. What kind of room did she want?

2. Did she have a reservation?

3. What did the receptionist ask the guest to do first?

Situation Four (Listening)

Situation: The lady who is checking out is not an ordinary customer. Listen
carefully and understand how Luke handles everything politely.

Words & Expressions	
hiccup	打嗝，暂时性的小问题
favorable	有利的，赞许的，良好的，顺利的，偏袒的

Task 1: Please choose a correct answer for each question.

1. Who was the guest impressed with?

A. The receptionist.   B. The chef.   C. The waitress.

2. How does the guest pay for her bill?

A. Credit card.   B. Check.   C. Cash.

3. What time does the lady's train leave?

A. 6:15 P. M.   B. 7:50 P. M.   C. 7:15 P. M.

4. How long does it take to get to the main station?

A. 50 minutes.   B. A quarter of an hour.   C. Half an hour.

Task 2: Listen to the dialogue again and try to fill in the blanks.

The female guest wanted to check out Room _____1_____ . She thought that the
conference was _____2_____ and enjoyed the dinner last night. She thought that their
staff coped with them very well. Particularly, the young waitress was a model of how
to handle difficult customers. She would report the successful meeting to her head office in _____3_____ . The woman would like to pay the extra bills by _____4_____ . Before
coming back home, the woman would like to enjoy a bit of _____5_____ .

Situation Five (Speaking)

Situation: After checking out, Tom found that he had left his wallet in the hotel, so he went back to the hotel to get his wallet back. The hotel
claimed that they had done the room cleaning and found nothing in
the hotel and the new customer had checked in. So Tom couldn't go

back to the room to check that by himself.

Task 1: In your opinion, does the hotel have responsibility in this case?

Useful Sentence Patterns

Expressions of Opinions	Expressions of Disagreement
I'm in favor of...	I don't think that...
I hold the idea that...	I'm opposed to the idea that...
My point of view is that...	I am against the idea that...
I argue that...	I disagreed the idea that...
I approve of the idea that...	I think it's not suitable that...

Task 2: Divide the class into two groups and one part is in support of the hotel and the other part is in support of the guest. Try to have a debate.

Situation Six (Speaking)

Situation: A guest called Mary came to a restaurant to have lunch.

Task 1: Suppose you are a waiter or waitress in the hotel and your partner acts as Mary. The following are the useful sentences for references.

1. Are you ready to order?
2. Would you like something to drink?
3. How many are you?

Task 2: A guest complains that there's a fly in his soup. Discuss with your partner about how to solve this kind of problem.

"A fly in your soup, eh? — Call
me if it gets any worse."

Situation Seven (Reading)

Situation: Everyone may have a chance to stay in a hotel in the future. You may have to choose the types of hotel you'd like to check in.

Task: Read the passage to get the idea about what types of hotel you may choose

according to different situations.

The Developing Process of the Hotel

The first hotels were very different from today's hotels. They were small inns built along the road. Later, as people began to travel by train, hotels were built in the centers of large cities. Usually located near railroad stations, these hotels were many stories tall and had hundreds of rooms. Although trains were a popular means of travel for some time, automobiles slowly began to take their place. Automobile travel caused problems for city hotels, which did not have parking space for so many cars. People who traveled by automobile needed a different kind of hotel. They needed places to stay that were near highways and had room to park. Motorists did not like to drive in heavy city traffic to reach a hotel. The answer to the motorists' problems came when a new kind of hotel was built. Motels were much smaller than hotels. Built on ground level, often in separate units, they were more convenient for people traveling. The separate units also made them quieter than hotels. Best of all, there was more than enough room for cars to park.

Nowadays, hotels (as well as other forms of accommodations) are generally **segmented**（划分）by the services and **amenities** （礼仪）offered. These two factors, along with location, also have a bearing on the price range.

Budget hotels offer clean **albeit**（虽然）simple rooms that provide the basics of places to sleep and shower. Usually budget hotels are designed for travelers looking to maximize their funds and minimize expenses. Prices can range from $20 per night to $70 per night.

Business hotels offer a high standard by providing rooms equipped with what business travelers would consider necessities. Usually found in business-class hotel rooms are high speed Internet connections, alarm clocks, comfortable beds, irons and ironing boards, coffee makers, **complimentary**（免费赠送的）newspaper delivery and hairdryers. Rates can range from $80 per night to $250 per night.

The facility of a business hotel would also offer an in-house restaurant, bar, exercise room and shuttle service to nearby airports. Limit concierge assistance is often included as well as room service, laundry and dry cleaning and wake-up calls.

Luxury hotels are known for their **lavish**（浪费的）decor and extraordinary service. With superior amenities, accommodations at luxury hotels are designed to thoroughly pamper and impress guests. According to a Business Week Online article, those in the luxury market are getting harder to please stating that luxury goods and service providers can't afford to **blunder**（弄糟）with the level of service and customer experience they provide. For this reason, many luxury hotels go far beyond the norm by providing a lifestyle experience equal to or better than what guests have become accustomed to at home.

Luxury hotels frequently offer full-service day spas, five-star restaurants staffed by world-class chefs, ballrooms, lavish pools, golf packages and guest services that are unsurpassed by any other class of hotel. In addition, luxury rooms generally include those amenities found in business-class hotels plus in-room safes, goose down comforters and pillows, marble showers and tubs, larger rooms, separate sitting or living area and fog-free bathroom mirrors. Rates can range from $129 per night to $2,000 per night.

Rates vary greatly depending on location and proximity to popular events and attractions.

There are other classifications of hotels, however, most will fall into one of these three or a combination of these three. With the lines between business and personal becoming more **blurred**(使……模糊), many entrepreneurs and business executives will attend conferences or embark on business trips with family in tow. Hotels are aware of this common occurrence and have become adept at providing facilities and services both business and **recreational**(休闲的)travelers enjoy.

Task 1: Getting a message.

After reading the passage, decide whether the following statements are true (T)or false(F).

1. The first hotels were built around the city centers.

2. Motels are usually small, high buildings built on the outskirts.

3. Business hotel are designed for travelers looking to maximize their funds and minimize expenses.

4. Hotel price is influenced by services, amenities and location.

Task 2: Skimming and scanning.

Scan the passage and answer the following questions.

1. What are the developing steps of hotel according to the passage?

_____

2. How are hotels classified into different types?

_____

3. After reading the passage, who are the major customers of each type of hotels?

_____

Task 3: Translate the following sentences into English.

1. 你只需填写一张表格就可以取得会员资格,它可以使你在买东西时享受打折的优惠。

2. 酒店豪华轿车服务(limousine)的最低消费为每 2 小时 240 人民币。

3. 我们公司提供一流的客房服务。

4. 团体预订我们有折扣。

Situation Eight (✏ Writing)

Situation: When we check in a hotel, the hotel always requires you to fill in a registration form to know some of your personal information and your personal requirement on the special things.

Task 1: **Before you enter the room, the receptionist asks you to fill in the registration form.**

登记表

登记表是将有关事项写在指定的表格上。内容填写应表述清楚。填写应据实。

Hotel Registration Form

Check-in Date _____

NAME _____

PHONE _____   FAX _____

ADDRESS _____

CITY _____   ZIP _____

NUMBER OF PEOPLE _____

NUMBER OF BEDS REQUESTED _____

ROOM TYPE * (see below)_____ SECOND CHOICE _____

ARRIVAL DATE ____/____/____ DEPARTURE DATE ____/____/____

All reservations must be guaranteed by a credit card or a deposit for the first night's room rate.

CREDIT CARD TYPE & NUMBER:

CREDIT CARD SIGNATURE:

CREDIT CARD EXPIRATION DATE:

ENCLOSED:

RESERVATIONS RECEIVED AFTER JANUARY 8, 2005, WILL BE PROVIDED ON A SPACE AVAILABLE BASIS.

PLEASE NOTE: In the event of cancellation, you must notify the Reservations Department fourteen (14) days prior to arrival. This will avoid a one-night no-show charge.

* ROOM TYPE SELECTIONS:

Oceanfront   @ $140 per room

Non-oceanfront   @ $125 per room

PLEASE RETURN THIS FORM TO

The King and Prince Beach & Golf Resort

Reservations Department

P. O. Box 20798

St. Simons Island, GA 31522   FAX: 912-638-7699

Task 2:This is a questionnaire made by Jerusalem Hotel. After staying in a hotel,
they require you to fill in the questionnaire.

调查

调查是对某人或某物进行客观的了解核查,以求对所调查的对象进行归纳、分析、比较以达到正确的认识。填写时应明确每一栏目的要求,客观地填写。

HOW WAS YOUR RESERVATION MADE?	
Wonderful Hotel Reservation Office ( )	Wonderful Hotel Website ( )
The Hotel Directly ( )	Other Website ( )
Group Reservation ( )	Airline ( )
Travel Agent ( )	Other Methods ( )
Was the information concerning your reservation correct? Yes( ) No( )	
Are you traveling on: Meeting / Conference/Individual Business/ Pleasure Combination / Pleasure	
* Your Name:	
Reply Address:	
* E-mail:	
Phone Number:	
Room No:	Date of Stay:
DURING YOUR VISIT	
Was your room clean and well maintained? Yes( ) No ( )	
Was the hotel clean and well maintained? Yes( ) No ( )	

（续表）

HOW WAS YOUR RESERVATION MADE?	
Was everything in your room in working order?	Yes( ) No ( )
Was the lighting in your room sufficient?	Yes( ) No ( )
Did we make you feel safe and secure?	Yes( ) No ( )
Did we handle your requests efficiently?	Yes( ) No ( )
Would you like to see anything added to your room?	Yes( ) No ( )
Whenever our staff interacted with you, did they present themselves in a pleasant and welcome manner?	Yes( ) No ( )
Perform their duties promptly and efficiently?	Yes( ) No ( )
Prove to be knowledgeable about the hotel and its services?	Yes( ) No ( )
Fulfill your requests and show commitment to your complete satisfaction?	Yes( ) No ( )
Will you want to come back and to recommend the hotel to others?	Yes( ) No ( )
How satisfied are you with your stay?	Unacceptable or Outstanding
Are there any suggestions or comments you would like to add?	

Self-evaluation

Situation	Standard of Evaluation	Grade			Difficulties and Suggestions
		Excellent	Good	Improved	
Situation 1 Situation 5-6	I can talk about the item freely in a real situation.				
Situation 2-4	I can listen clearly and understand quickly.				
Situation 7	I can get its gist in limited time. I can translate related sentences and the short passage well.				
Situation 8	I can write a practical passage about the registration form and questionnaire.				

Item Ten　　　Music

Competence Objectives

1. Students can know some musical instruments.
2. Students can talk about great musicians domestic and abroad.
3. Students can know some special concerts.
4. Students can get some information about awards in the music industry.
5. Students can learn some musicals.
6. Students can talk about their favorite singers.
7. Students can know the importance of music.
8. Students can write notes in English.

Warm-up Activities

After looking through the following pictures, please name these musical instruments in English. Try your best to list more instruments.

Situation One (Discussing)

Situation: It is the first time that the music club's members gather together. The president of the club shows the students some pictures related to some great musicians on the blackboard.

Task: You like the music very much, and you are one member of the club, too. Now you can select one of following pictures and then introduce him or her to other students. The following information is for reference.

1. The Three Tenors is a name given to the Spanish singers Placido Domingo and Jose Carreras and the Italian singer Luciano Pavarotti.

2. Anne-Sophie Mutter (born June 29, 1963) is a German violin virtuoso.

Situation Two (Listening)

Situation: The New Year is approaching. On that day Mary and her parents like to watch the Vienna Philharmonic New Year's Concert broadcast by television. Now Mary and her father are talking about the Concert.

Words & Expressions

philharmonic	交响乐团	contemporary	同时代的人,同龄人
nostalgic	乡愁的;怀旧的	ambassador	大使,使节
repertoire	全部节目;保留剧目	Johann Strauss	约翰·施特劳斯
the Vienna Philharmonic New Year's Concert		维也纳新年音乐会	

Task 1：Listen to their conversation. And then try to answer the following questions according to the dialogue. The conversation will be spoken twice.

1. How many countries broadcast the Concert on New Year's Day?

_____

2. Did the Philharmonic play the works of the Johann Strauss family?

_____

3. What does the Concert want to send people all over the world?

_____

Task 2：Listen to their conversation again. Exchange the information on the Vienna Philharmonic New Year's Concert with your partner. Then give a brief introduction of it to the whole class.

Situation Three (🔊 Listening)

Situation: The annual Grammy Awards is coming. Bob and Alice are talking
about it in the office.

Words & Expressions			
prominent	杰出的,突出的	variation	变动,变化
Oscar	奥斯卡	phonograph	留声机,电唱机
trophy	奖品	telecast	以电视广播传播

Task 1: **Listen to the dialogue and decide whether the following statements are
true (T) or false (F).**

1. They are talking about the annual Grammy Awards Ceremony.

2. The Grammy is one of the most prominent award ceremonies in the world.

3. All of the musicians in the US are very proud of winning the trophy.

4. The Grammy cup is like an old phonograph.

5. The first Grammy Award telecast took place in 1950.

Task 2: **Listen to the conversation again. And then try to answer the following
questions according to the dialogue.**

1. Is it said that Grammy is like Oscar in the music industry? Why or why not?

_____

2. When did the first Grammy Award telecast take place?

_____

3. What does the Grammy Award praise for?

_____

Situation Four (Listening)

Situation： Tomorrow is a weekend. Jack will invite Alice to see a musical
named The *Sound of Music*. On the way to the cinema，Jack tells
Alice the information related to the film.

Words & Expressions			
novice	新信徒,新手	nun	尼姑，修女
governess	女家庭教师	box-office	票房
widower	鳏夫	the Nazis	纳粹
household	家庭的，家喻户晓的		

Task 1: **You will hear Jack's descriptions of the film, but with some words or phrases missing. Listen carefully. After the second reading, you are required to fill in the missing words or phrases according to what you have heard. The material will be spoken twice. Before you listen, learn the above words and expressions.**

The Sound of Music, a feature-film musical about a young _____ novice working as a governess who brings _____ and _____ to a widower's large family, set in Austria during World War II. Released in 1965 and based on _____ events, this box-office hit earned Academy Awards for best picture, best director, best film editing, best _____, and best musical score. Julie Andrews stars as Maria, the novice nun who, on the advice of her Mother Superior, takes a job as a _____ in the _____ of Captain Von Trapp (played by Christopher Plummer), _____ his seven children, while she considers her vocation. Maria teaches the children to sing, and she and the captain begin to _____. When the Nazis _____ Austria, Von Trapp and his family, including Maria, flee the country. The film was an adaptation of the stage show written by Richard Rodgers and Oscar Hammerstein II and first produced in 1959; the songs include "Do Re Mi" and "My Favorite Things" are popular till now.

Task 2: **Listen again and try your best to retell Jack's descriptions of the musical.**

Situation Five (⟷Speaking)

Situation: After having the whole class, Betty and her roommates are discussing their favorite singers.

Task: **You are Betty's roommate. Work in pairs and then describe the singer you like best. The following is the information for reference.**

1. He has a soft and charming voice and excellent singing skills.

2. ... is my favorite Hong Kong pop star.

3. He can handle many different styles of music very well, such as pop, rock, Jazz, R&B, etc.

4. Sometimes he is a songwriter for his own music albums.

5. What attracts me most is...

6. Besides, he is good at live performance.

7. My favorite singer is...

8. Her first album is..., songs from this album such as... and... are very popular in young men.

9. Now all of his fans, including me, are crazy about both his handsome and talent!

Situation Six (Reading)

Situation: What would life be without music? The world would be a very quiet place. Music can be a way to deliver messages, a poetic medium, a fine art, or nothing more than a source of entertainment. No matter what it is used for, music is the perfect art and it is very important for all of us.

Task: Read the passage to get a general idea of the importance of music, and then finish the tasks.

The Importance of Music

Music plays an important part in all cultures. People use music in ceremonies, in work, and in personal and social activities.

In ceremonies. Nearly all people use music in their religious services. One kind of religious music seeks to create a state of mystery. For example, some cultures have special musical instruments played only by **priests** (牧师) on important occasions, such as harvest ceremonies and the **burials** (葬礼)of chiefs. Similarly, much Western church music attempts to create a feeling of distance from the daily world. Other religious music helps produce a sense of participation among **worshipers** (崇拜者). The singing of **hymns** (赞美诗,圣歌) by a **congregation** (宗教等的集会) is a good example of this function of religious music.

Many nonreligious ceremonies and **spectacles** (值得看的东西) also use music. They include sports events, graduations, **circuses** (马戏;马戏团), parades, and the **crowning** (加冕) of kings and queens.

In work. Before machines became important, people had to do much difficult or boring work by hand. Laborers sang songs to help make their work seem easier. For example, crews aboard sailing ships sang **chanteys** (船歌), songs with a strong, regular **beat** (拍子). Today, the wide use of machines has made the singing of work songs rare in industrialized societies. However, many offices and factories provide background music for workers.

In personal and social activities. Many people perform music for their own satisfaction. Singing in a **chorus** (合唱队) of playing a musical instrument in a band can be very enjoyable. Music provides people with a way to express their feelings. A group of happy campers may sing cheerful songs as they sit around a **campfire** (营火,篝火). A sad person may play a **mournful** (悲哀的)tune on a guitar.

People use music at a variety of social occasions. At parties and dinners, music is often played for dancing or simply for listening. In some countries, a young man shows that a young woman is special to him by serenading her or by sending musicians to play and sing for her.

Task 1: Skimming.

Decide whether the following statements are true(T)or false(F) after skimming the passage.

1. People use music in ceremonies, in work, and in personal and social activities.

2. All people use music in their religious services.

3. One of the functions of religious music is to create a feeling of participation.

4. Today, the wide use of machines has made the singing of work songs rare in societies.

5. If a young man wants to express his special feeling toward a young woman, he will sing a love song for her.

Task 2: Translate the sentences into English.

1. 人们用音乐表达感情和思想。

2. 音乐是很多文化和社会活动的重要组成部分。

3. 音乐让人娱乐和放松。

4. 人应该是从有语言开始就可能已经懂得唱歌了。

5. 西方音乐有两大类——古典的和流行的。

Task 3: Discuss the following topics with your partner.

1. Do you know the classification of music? And what are they?

2. What kinds of music do you like best? Can you introduce them to your friends?

Situation Seven (✑ Writing)

Situation: You want to go to Lee Hom's concert with Li. But he isn't in while you arrive at his dorm, so you leave a note for him.

Tuesday

Dear Li,

I have two tickets for Lee Hom's concert. I'm very glad to invite you to come with me. I'm sure we will have a very happy time and enjoy ourselves thoroughly. Would you like to come on time at 5:00 P. M. today, at the gate of the Grand Theatre?

Zhang Yang

Task 1: After reading it, you're expected to talk to your partner about how to write notes in English.

便条

便条是一种简单的书信。虽然内容简单,但却有其独特的风格。主要目的是为了尽快地把最新的信息、通知、要求或者活动的时间、地点转告给对方。便条可以有题目,也可以省略题目。便条开篇须有称呼语,但称呼可以比较随便。日期部分可写在便条的右上角。日期的签署通常只需写星期几或星期几的上午或下午,也可只写上午或下午和具体时间。只写日期也可以。便条结尾须署上留条人的姓名,位置在正文的右下角。便条的形式和内容简洁,故可以用几句话概括。文内语言尽量通俗、口语化,简单扼要,直截了当,无须使用客套语言。便条虽简单,但中心务必突出,更要注明活动的时间及地点。便条不需要邮寄,不用信封。通常请人代为转交。有时可写在留言板和留言簿上。

便条内容和类型不尽相同,可以灵活变通。但各类便条必须包括以下几个基本要素:

(1)便条日期(Date);

(2)称呼(Salutation);

(3)正文(Body);

(4)署名(Signature).

Useful Sentence Patterns

1. I shall feel obliged if you will favor me with a call at your earliest convenience.

   如您方便,请早日来电,我将不胜感激。

2. Delighted! Will call at 2 P. M. tomorrow.

   来条收悉,定于明天下午两点拜访。

3. I shall be very happy to call at your house at 6:30 this evening. Until then...

   我定于今晚 6:30 去你家,望等候。

4. Upon receiving this note, please come to my office.

   见条后,请立即来我办公室。

5. Mr. Lee stands in urgent need of your service.

   李先生急需你的帮助。

6. Your note with an admission ticket enclosed is much appreciated.

   留言和一张入场券均已收到,不胜感激。

7. I'm very grateful to you for your kind invitation, and I'm sure to come to see your concert.

   承蒙邀请观看你们的音乐会,我一定按时到场。

8. Please accept this little gift as a small token of my esteem for you.

奉上这小小的礼物，以表达我对您的崇高敬意。

9. I trust my absence will not cause you any serious inconvenience.

望我的缺席不会给你带来太大的不便。

10. Please favor me with an early reply.

敬请早复。

11. Hoping that the matter will be dealt with as soon as possible.

希望能及早处理此事。

Task 2: Leave a note to your mother, as you are in a hurry to take part in the English Evening Party in school.

Self-evaluation

Situation	Standard of Evaluation	Grade			Difficulties and Suggestions
		Excellent	Good	Improved	
Situation 1 Situation 5	I can talk about the item freely in a real situation.				
Situation 2-4	I can listen clearly and understand quickly.				
Situation 6	I can get its gist in limited time. I can translate related sentences and the short passage well.				
Situation 7	I can write a practical passage about a note.				

Item Eleven   Getting the Job

Competence Objectives

1. Students can know how to make preparation for job-hunting.
2. Students can learn about some job-hunting channels.
3. Students can know how to position themselves in job-hunting.
4. Students can talk about some tips in interview.
5. Students can learn some usually-used questions and answers in interview.
6. Students can know how to search for a job online.
7. Students can learn how to cope with the difficulties in job-hunting.

Warm-up Activities

What qualities do companies look for when they are hiring a person? Look at the following lists and check (√) the five most important qualities for each job.

(Secretary)

(Import/Export manager)

(Attorney)

(Delivery driver)

Qualities	Secretary	Import/Export Manager	Attorney	Delivery Driver
Experience				
Good communication skills				
Honesty and integrity				
Lots of confidence				
Problem-solving skills				
Qualifications				
Professional appearance				
Strong leadership skills				

Situation One (Discussing)

Situation：Soon you will leave your college, and everyone wants to find a good job. Before hunting for a job, what kind of preparation you should make?

Task：Now discuss this question with your partners.

Situation Two (◀ Listening)

Situation： Xiao Hong has just left her college and wants to find a job, but she doesn't know how to hunt for a good job. Lots of newly-graduated students are unaware of the importance of learning about channels of searching for a job.

Task：You will hear a short passage. The passage will be read only twice. After the second reading, you are required to finish the following match exercises according to what you have heard. Now the passage will begin.

Words & Expressions

utilize	使用，利用
relevant	有关的，相应的
available	可用到的，可利用的，有用的，有空的，接受探访
represent	表现，描绘，声称，象征，扮演，回忆，再赠
deadline	最终期限
sponsor	发起人，主办者，保证人，主办人
navigate	航行，航海，航空

Column A

1. (　　) On-campus interviewing program.

2. (　　) Job listing on line.

3. (　　) Job listings in print.

4. (　　) Job fairs.

Column B

a. Not for the shy and retiring.

b. Opportunities to speak with many employers at one time in one space.

c. Career Services during business hours.

d. You'll find some jobs that you won't find online.

e. You need patience to navigate a variety of sites and read listings.

f. You can view them at 2：00 A. M. if you feel like.

g. Not every industry or type of job is represented.

h. Easy to publish your resume.

Situation Three (◀Listening)

Situation：For some college students，career objective setting requires careful self-exploration and planning to find careers that coincide with（与……相符）their temperament（气质,性情），long term goals，and lifestyle expectations. One expert will give us some suggestions. What he has said maybe help us.

Task：**Listen to a short passage. The passage will be read twice. After the second reading，you are required to fill in the missing words according to what you have heard. Now the passage will begin.**

Establishing Goals

By carefully planning your career，you can determine：

• interests and strengths；

• short-term objectives and long-term goals；

• education needed；

• occupations that match your skills and interests；

• corporate culture and values that will be right for you；

• future lifestyle.

Think of establishing your goals as a three-step process：self-reflection，self-assessment，and career orientation.

1. Self-reflection

Self-reflection involves thinking about personal _____ ，such as values，and how you fit into the world. These values determine how you _____ and what you think is important and influence your relationships and your career path.

2. Self-assessment

Self-assessment requires that you evaluate your _____ and interests in the light of your career goal. Do you have the interests and aptitudes for the work you have chosen? How can you approach your job to make it satisfying?

3. Career Orientation

How can you stay on the right career path? Developing focused short-term objectives and _____ goals will _____ you to develop a career plan that will orient you as you travel to your destination.

Situation Four (Listening)

Situation: It's your turn! As the interview comes to a close, one of the final questions you may be asked is "What can I answer you?" If you have interview questions of your own being ready to ask, you aren't simply trying to get this job—you are also interviewing the employer to assess whether this company and the position are a good fit for you. The following free talk between an interviewer and an interviewee will let you understand how to ask and answer questions in an interview.

Task: Listen to the conversation and complete the conversation by filling in the missing words. The conversation will be spoken twice.

Interviewer: What kind of a person do you think you are?

Interviewee: Well, I am always energetic and _____. That is my strongest personality.

Interviewer: What are your strengths and _____?

Interviewee: Em, as I have said, I am diligent and industrious. On the other hand, sometimes I'm too hard-working and I put myself under too much pressure to make things perfect.

Interviewer: What qualities would you expect of persons working as a team?

Interviewee: To work in a team, in my opinion, two characteristics are necessary for a person. That is, the person must be _____ and aggressive.

Interviewer: How do you spend your _____ time?

Interviewee: I like playing games and having sports. They are my favorite hobbies.

Interviewer: So, what kind of sport do you like most?

Interviewee: Oh, it's hard to narrow it down to just one. I mean, I like all kinds of sports, basketball, swimming, bike riding and so on.

Maybe it is just the reason why I am so _____ and vigorous.

Situation Five (⟷Speaking)

Situation:Job interviewing never seems to get any easier—even when you have gone on more interviews than you can count. You are meeting new people, selling yourself and your skills, and often being asked what you know or don't know. Guo Qihong, an experienced HR manager was invited to our college to give us a lecture about job interview tips to help prepare you for an interview effectively.

Task:**After listening to her lecture,discuss with your classmates in groups and report your ideas in class. The following lecture script will help you.**

Preparing for Your Interview

Interview is somewhat like giving a presentation: if it is to be informative and successful, the speaker must be prepared. At an interview, you are the speaker and arriving with a composed, self-confident attitude can help you to show the employer your readiness to do the job. Here are some tips on how to win the competition.

1. Do your research about the company

Never walk into an interview without knowing about the products and services provided by the company. Find out about its corporate culture and future projects so that you can demonstrate how you can contribute to the company as it continues to grow. Have a solid understanding about its mission and values so that you can inquire about the company's aims. For more information about researching companies, visit *Researching Companies* on this site.

2. Plan your schedule

Find out the exact location of the office where you will be interviewed and make plans to arrive at least 15 minutes before the interview. If you must, look up bus schedules or plan alternate routes if you anticipate traffic jams. It is impossible to recover from a late arrival at your interview, so avoid being late altogether.

3. Dress appropriately

Dress a notch above your day-to-day work attire. For example, if everyone wears blue jeans to work, arrive in dress slacks and a sport shirt (for men) or in a skirt and a blouse (for women). If applying for a job in an office environment, both men and women should wear a business suit.

4. Rehearse

Prepare a list of interview questions you can expect to be asked at an interview. Know what you are going to say before the interview. To prepare best, write down your answers, and go over the information several times the day before the interview. Ask a friend or relative to assist as you practice answering those questions in a mock interview.

Despite all the practice, however, always anticipate questions you did not expect to be asked. Such questions help to demonstrate your adaptability and ability to think on the spot.

5. Prepare

Prepare two or three questions to ask the interviewer. The questions should seek some specific information about the responsibilities of the job, future projects, and organizational structure.

Here are some key questions you can ask during an interview.

- What are the day-to-day responsibilities of the person in this position?
- Why is this position open?
- What is the career path for this position in this company?
- Where does this position fit into the overall organizational structure of the company?
- Are there important changes such as expansion of products or services, which will affect my position?
- Are the procedures of the position completely developed or is a person encouraged to contribute innovative new ideas?

Situation Six (⬌ Speaking)

Situation: For a creative and practical job seeker, the Internet is an important tool in reaching employers after you have conducted thorough employment research. If your friend wants to use the technology and the Internet to enhance his chances of getting the job he wants, can you give your friend some tips about job searching online?

Task: **Now discuss the situation with your classmates, and then present your ideas before class.**

Situation Seven (⟐ Reading)

Situation: It's not easy for the newly-graduated college students to get an ideal job nowadays. Then what's the appropriate attitudes towards career and job, how to make use of relationship around you, and how to cope with the frustration in the process of your job-hunting, some suggestions are given to you.

Task：Read the passage and get the general idea about it and then finish the tasks.

If You Can't Get a Job Right Away, Don't Despair

Pick a Career Instead of a Job

Looking for a job **haphazardly**(偶然地)，because you majored in something or because you saw a listing that looks somewhat interesting，you'll risk getting started in a career that holds no real **appeal**（吸引力)for you，and then you'll have to leave it to find something else. Why not plan your career **strategically**（颇有策略地)，just like you planned your education?

Start by doing a self-assessment that teaches you things about yourself that you might never have thought about——for example，what you like and don't like in a work environment，what defines success for you，and what type of work would make you want to sit in traffic for hours just for the **privilege**(特权) of showing up. Knowing these things can help you **determine**(确定)which occupations(职业)could be a good fit for you.

If You Can't Get a Job Right Away, Don't Despair

If you start thinking of yourself as a victim or allow yourself to **lapse**(堕落)into **prolonged**(延长的) **negativity**(消极)，you won't be hurting anyone except yourself. Worrying until you get sick，**abusing**(滥用) drugs or denying that you've reached an **impasse**(僵局) won't help either. The best strategy for moving on is to recognize the reality of the situation，**acknowledge**(承认) your feelings and find a way to cope productively. Reach out to your support systems，and consider taking some time off——after all，you'll never have the freedom of being between school and work again!

Building up Network in Your Chosen Field

A huge **percentage**(比率)of job openings aren't advertised because employers prefer to hire people through word of mouth. Developing relationships with people working in your field，then，means that you're top of mind whenever they hear of a new opportunity.

Learn about new contacts by researching firms in your industry，joining social networking sites like LinkedIn，asking your parents' friends，and joining relevant professional associations. Approach individuals by e-mail first，and don't put them on the defensive by asking for a job **outright**(直率地). Instead，show curiosity about their career path and see if they'll agree to lunch or coffee.

Establish Your Reputation(名声) as a Can-Do, Enthusiastic Employee

Don't have a sense of entitlement—— your company isn't responsible for your career growth：you are. Only approach your boss with a problem or complaint if you've explored all options for resolving it yourself. When you do, be prepared with a solution you could **implement**(实施) with her help.

The words I don't have time should never escape from your lips. If you know something needs to be done, do it without being **prodded**(刺激). Your boss will quickly come to see you as someone he can count on and a huge asset to the team. If you have **conflicting**(冲突的) **priorities**(优先), ask your boss to help sort them out.

Don't Think of Your First Job as the Be All, End All to Stardom

How can you master the skills it takes to get ahead without putting any time in the trenches(战壕)? That's like saying you could win an Olympic medal in swimming without learning to doggie **paddle**(戏水) first. Look at your first post-college positions as **temporary**(暂时的) stops on your career path instead of **permanent** (永久性的) ones. Don't be in such a rush to get promoted either— you have a long career life ahead of you to shoulder the heavy burden of being on top. In the meantime, enjoy getting paid to learn everything you can so that **snagging**(清除障碍物) your next job isn't quite as challenging!

Task 1: Getting a message.

Fill in the blanks with the missing words in the passage.

1. Pick a _____ instead of a _____.

2. If you can't get a job right away, don't _____.

3. Building up _____ in your chosen field.

4. Establish your _____ as a Can-Do, enthusiastic employee.

5. Don't think of your first job as the be all, end all to _____.

Task 2: Skimming and scanning.

Scan the passage and answer the following questions.

1. What's the harm of looking for a job haphazardly?

_____

2. What's the best strategy when you can't get a job as expected?

_____

3. Why should you try to develop relationships in your field?

_____

4. What kind of image and reputation should you establish in the company? Why?

_____

5. How to understand the relation between your first job and your long career goal?

_____

Task 3: Translate the following into English.

1. 不要随便找一个工作，否则你可能会很快换工作，因为这个工作对你缺乏吸引力。

2. 在你的专业领域建立广泛的人际关系意味着你有更多的机会。

3. 是你自己而不是公司会为你的职业发展负责。

4. 做一个自我评估会让你知道哪种职业适合你。

5. 你大学后的第一份工作只是你职业道路上临时的一站。

Situation Eight (✍ Writing)

Situation: You are hunting for a job and the following is an ad you read in newspaper. Read it and finish the tasks below.

A Job Wanted Ad

Whirpool Corporation/Company is a famous manufacturer and marketer of electrical home appliances, with it's headquarters in Tianjin. It has more than 20 branches over the country. We are/The company is seeking for one sales manager now.

Qualifications:

- Chinese citizen, aged 35-40.
- With college diploma in Marketing, Economics or related field
- Minimum of 5 years' experiences in sales management
- Proficiency in English speaking and writing
- Willing to travel frequently
- Good at using a computer.

Those interested please contact Mr. John Smith at 24876669.

Task 1: Answer the following questions.

1. What is the vacant position in the company?

_____

2. What are the qualifications required?

_____

Task 2: The following is a job vacancy advertisement of Castle Hotel, written in Chinese. You are required to make an English version of it.

Castle Hotel 系峨眉山旅游公司直属的五星级宾馆，现招聘一名热心的工作人员，协助宾馆扩大业务。申请人需具有宾馆工作的全面经验及至少一年的助理经验。应聘人须熟练掌握英语及另外两种语言。

待遇：高额工资、奖金、享受节假日，员工在公司内有良好的晋升前景。

申请时请携带个人简历及近期照片一张，交到 Gerry Bateman 处。

地址：中国四川峨眉山人民路 29 号

电话：0833-5526888

Words & Expressions			
applicant	申请人	奖金	bonus
promotion	晋升		

Useful Phrases and Sentence Patterns

1. Wanted/ A Job Wanted Ad/ A Help Wanted Ad.

   招聘广告。

2. We are/The company is seeking...

   现招聘……

3. We are seeking an intelligent and aggressive individual with the desire to make a career in...

   现招聘一名以……为其职业且能干、有进取心的人。

4. Qualifications/Requirement.

   条件

5. A minimum college degree.

   大专以上学历。

6. Some experience with/in ... would be an advantage.

   有……工作经验者优先。

7. Salary is negotiable.

   工资面议。

8. Please submit a resume both in Chinese and English.

   请提供中英文简历。

9. Application in English and Chinese with a resume and a recent photograph should reach us by 25 July, 2005.

   申请用中英文书写并附简历和一张近照，于 2005 年 7 月 25 日前寄来。

10. Application deadline.

    申请截止日期。

11. Those interested please contact ... at 24876669.

    有意者请拨打电话 24876669 与……联系。

Self-evaluation

Situation	Standard of Evaluation	Grade			Difficulties and Suggestions
		Excellent	Good	Improved	
Situation 1 Situation 5-6	I can talk about the item freely in a real situation.				
Situation 2-4	I can listen clearly and understand quickly.				
Situation 7	I can get its gist in limited time. I can translate related sentences and the short passage well.				
Situation 8	I can write a practical passage about an ad.				

Item Twelve   Doing the Job

Competence Objectives

1. Students can understand the company organizational chart and know responsibilities of each department.

2. Students can talk about what to do in a real position.

3. Students can give job descriptions.

4. Students can give product presentation in English.

5. Students can learn how to make a market survey and negotiate with customers and clients.

6. Students can ask for and give instructions on how to use something.

7. Students can know how to improve job satisfaction.

8. Students can write inquiries and offers in English.

Warm-up Activities

Do you know the following logos? What companies and enterprises they represent for? Tell your partner which of them is your favorite and why?

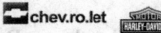

Situation One (Discussing)

Situation: Mr. James Bond is a new managing assistant in a chemical joint venture. Now he is studying the organization chart of the enterprise carefully with the office secretary. By understanding the organizational chart, he believes that he can have some ideas on how to fit into the company and what types of jobs are available.

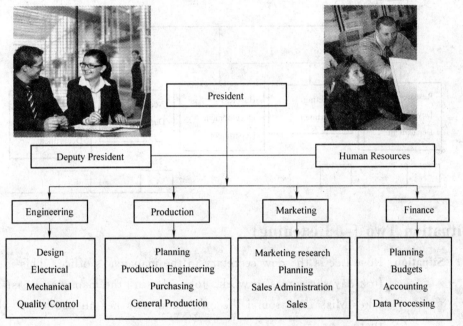

Task 1: Now discuss with your partner the following questions.

1. What is a corporate structure?
2. What are the functions of a company structure?
3. List four purposes of an organizational chart.

Task 2: Match the responsibilities to different departments.

A. to handle all financial matters
B. to market the goods and services produced for consumers
C. to make sure policy is implemented and advise the board of management
D. in charge of company strategy and general policy
E. to take care of new product development
F. in charge of personnel

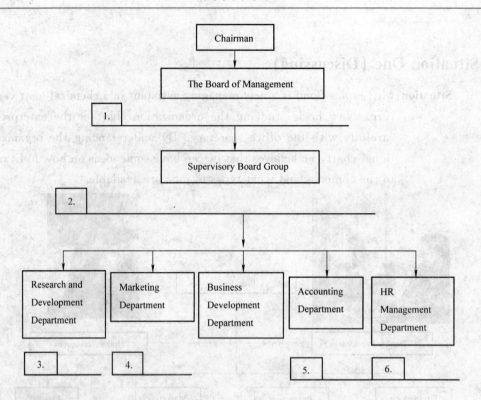

Situation Two (Listening)

Situation: Rose Lee is the new secretary in the manager's office. This is the first day she comes to work. John Martin, the managing assistant, takes Miss Lee around the office and tells her all about her work there.

Task: Listen to the conversation. Fill in the chart below according to the conversation and then compare your answers with your partner. The conversation will be spoken twice.

Words & Expressions	
routine 惯例;例行公事	pick up 学会
cupboard 柜子;橱柜	carbon paper 复写纸
cabinet 陈列柜	electric typewriter 电子打字机
alphabetically 按字母排序	essential 必备的;极其重要的
shorthand 速记	confidential file 机要文件

Office Items	Where	What to Do (tick)		Work Time
an electric typewriter		use an electric typewriter		
		file letters alphabetically		
all letters		keep the confidential file in the safe		
		take the clients into the office		
	in the cupboard	work with samples		
		do accounting work		
		take notes in shorthand		

Situation Three (🔊 Listening)

Situation: Janet and Peter used to be schoolmates. Two years ago they graduated from college and haven't seen each other since then. They bump into each other at today's business party.

Task 1: **Listen to them talking about their jobs. As you listen, fill in the table below and then compare your answers with your partner. The conversation will be read only twice.**

Words & Expressions	
What a coincidence! 真巧!	to be responsible for 负责
computer technician 电脑技术人员	stressful 紧张的;有压力的
day-to-day basis 按每日	coordinate 协调
administration 行政管理	transportation 交通
in-house 室内	need-to-know basis 按需要
accommodation 住宿	demanding 很费心的
entertainment 娱乐	

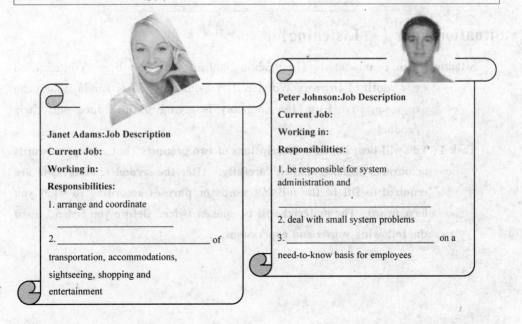

Janet Adams:Job Description
Current Job:
Working in:
Responsibilities:
1. arrange and coordinate
_____
2. _____ of
transportation, accommodations,
sightseeing, shopping and
entertainment

Peter Johnson:Job Description
Current Job:
Working in:
Responsibilities:
1. be responsible for system
administration and
_____
2. deal with small system problems
3. _____ on a
need-to-know basis for employees

Task 2：Give definitions to the following jobs. Take the first one as an example.

1. A construction worker：

a worker who makes something, especially buildings, bridges, etc.

2. A mechanic：

_____

3. An electrical engineer：

_____

4. A firefighter：

_____

5. A flight attendant：

_____

6. A computer programmer：

_____

7. An accountant：

_____

8. A social worker：

_____

9. An animation designer：

_____

10. A quality inspector：

_____

Situation Four (Listening)

Situation：You're now at the Guangzhou 2009 Spring Trade Fair. You come to the booth of Browny Wooden Toy Company. Miss Linda Blair, the representative from the company is trying to introduce you their products.

Task 1：You will hear Linda's descriptions of two products, but with some words or phrases missing. Listen carefully. After the second reading, you are required to fill in the missing words or phrases according to what you have heard. The material will be spoken twice. Before you listen, learn the following words and expressions.

Words & Expressions

wag 摇摆;摇动	tinkle 发叮当声
rotate 旋转	jiggle (使)左右摇摆
toddler 刚学步的小孩	fabulous 棒极了
gorgeous 极好的	
rubber trimmed wheels 橡胶滚边的轮子	

This _____ pull along wood toy has _____ that wags, eyes that roll and a tongue that _____ . His ears can be rotated and his head jiggles as he is _____ on his rubber trimmed wheels. Browny comes nicely boxed and makes it a fabulous special occasion or first birthday _____ for both boys and girls. The price is _____ .

Another _____ baby gift, this gorgeous little _____ toy pulled along is just the thing to accompany babies and toddlers _____ about the house. We love droopy ears and the bell (hidden safely inside) that _____ tinkles when he is on the move. Hand made, _____ and beautifully packaged. The price is _____ .

Task 2: Listen again and tick the number of the toys she is describing.

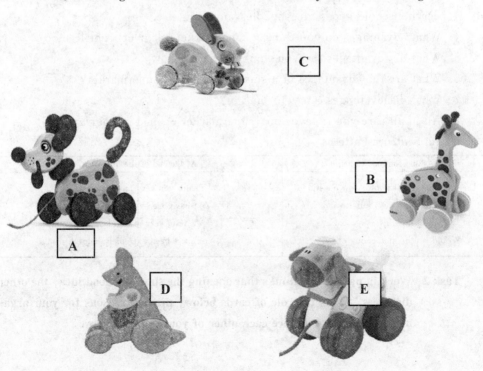

Situation Five (👄Speaking)

Situation: You're working in the Quake Company. Your company is expanding and is planning to buy a plot of land in a small town centre, with the aim of building a large supermarket and a western style fast-food restaurant. Before completing the plan, you're sent first to carry out a market survey among the people in the area to find out if there will be a demand for such a store. And then negotiate with people in the town.

Task 1: Work in groups of five or six, one of whom should play the role of researcher, interview different people by using the following questionnaire.

Market Research Survey

1. Have you ever been shopping in a supermarket?　　　　　　　Yes/No
2. If one is opened in your town, would you shop there?　　　　Yes/No
3. What do you buy from the supermarket?

   groceries, toys, fruit, frozen food, meat, clothes, bread, stationery, wine and beer, household goods, rice, noodles, anything else.
4. What advantages do you think a supermarket has over a small shop?
5. What disadvantages can you think of?
6. What are the advantages of a small shop over a supermarket?
7. What disadvantages can you think of?
8. All in all, are you in favor of a supermarket opened in your area?

Useful Sentence Patterns

Asking someone to help	At the end of the interview
Do you mind if I ask you a few questions?	Thank you very much indeed.
Could you spare me a minute and...?	You have been very cooperative.
Could I possibly ask you...?	I am very grateful...
Would you be kind enough to ...?	You have been extremely helpful.

Task 2: Work in pairs. One thinks that opening the shop is a good idea, the other disagrees. Using the role of cards below, prepare reasons for your argument and try to convince each other of your point of view.

Card A

   You are the representative of the big company. You are talking to people from the neighborhood committee. Try to convince them that the fast-food restaurant would be a good idea. Some reasons might be:

1. It will create new jobs.
2. It will make good, fast food available to people in the neighborhood.
3. The shop will offer nutritious food. (good for your health)
4. The building is attractive and modern.
5. There will be a playground in the back where children can play.

...

Card B

   You live in a neighborhood where a fast-food restaurant will be built. You and your neighbors do not want the restaurant. Talk to the representative of the company and tell them why you don't think the restaurant is a good idea. Some reasons might be:

1. The building is ugly.
2. The area around the restaurant will be very noisy.
3. Everything they cook is fried and unhealthy that is not good for you.
4. There will be a lot of rubbish. This may attract rats and make the neighborhood smell bad.
5. There are enough places to eat lunch already.

...

Situation Six (Speaking)

Situation: The Personnel Department at Timber has just bought a new photocopier. The secretary, Jenny, has no idea of how to use it. Helen in the Manager's Office gives her some instructions.

Task 1: Practice the following dialogue in roles. Pay special attention to all the expressions that Helen uses to explain the steps in using the photocopier.

Jenny: Excuse me, Helen, I wonder if you can show me how to use the photocopier.

Helen: Sure.

Jenny: Tell me what I have to do first?

Helen: First, turn on the photocopier and check the paper tray to ensure that there's enough paper in it. Remember to wait a couple of minutes for the copier to warm up.

Jenny: All right. And what's next.

Helen: Next, lift the lid of the photocopier and place the document that you want to copy face down. Place the lid of the photocopier slowly down to hold the document in place. Choose the number of copies that you want.

Jenny: Oh, I see. And then in the end, you just press the "Start" or "Copy" button on the top. The document will be copied.

Helen: That's it.

Jenny: But what if paper or documents become jammed during photocopying?

Helen: Well, if that happens, press the stop button, remove the jammed paper and start again.

Jenny: OK, I think I can manage that. Thanks a lot, Helen.

Task 2: **Work in pairs. Match the names of equipment with the pictures. And then, choose one of the pictures below, give instructions.**

a scanner, a photocopier, a digital camera, a laser printer, a shredder, a laptop, a projector, a fax machine

1._____ 2. _____ 3. _____ 4. _____

5._____ 6. _____ 7. _____ 8. _____

Situation Seven (Reading)

Situation: Your good friend Li Qiang found his job in a company a year ago. But recently he tells you that he's leaving the company because he can never gain satisfaction from his work. As it is not easy to find new jobs at the time of economic crisis. You suggest that he should go to a career expert for help before he leaves. Let's see what the career expert will say to him.

Task: **Read the passage to get a general idea of what strategies the career expert has developed to improve job satisfaction.**

Strategies to Improve Your Job Satisfaction

Depending on the basic cause of your dissatisfaction, there may be several ways to increase your job satisfaction.

Stay positive

Positive attitude is one of the most **effective**(有效的,有影响的) ways to gain satisfaction from your work. Use positive thinking to **reframe**(再构造) your thoughts about your job. Change your attitude about work, so it won't necessarily happen overnight. Once you're **alert**(警觉的,留心的) to the ways you think of job brings you down, you can improve your job satisfaction. Try these **techniques**(技术;技巧).

Stop negative thoughts

Pay attention to the messages you give to yourself. When you catch yourself thinking your job is terrible, stop the thought in its tracks.

Put things in perspective(远景,看法)

Remember, everyone experiences good days and bad days in the job. Look for the **silver lining**(一线希望). "Reframing" can help you find the good in a bad situation. For example, you receive a less than perfect performance **evaluation**(估价,评价) and your boss warns you to improve or move to another job. Instead of taking it personally or looking for another job right away, look for the silver lining. Depending on where you work, the silver lining may be attending continuing education classes, working closely with a performance **coach**(指导者,教练) and having the satisfaction of showing your boss you're **capable**(有能力的) of change.

Learn from your mistakes

Failure is one of the greatest learning tools, but many people let failure defeat them. When you make a mistake at work, learn from it and try again.

Be grateful(感激的,感谢的)

Gratitude(感激之情) can help you focus on what's positive about your job. Ask yourself, "What am I grateful for at work today?" If it's only that you're having lunch with a trusted co-worker, that's OK. But find at least one thing you're grateful for and **savor**(体验) it.

Whether your work is a job, a career or a calling, you can take steps to **restore**(恢复) meaning to your job. Make the best of difficult work situations by being positive. Doing so will help you manage your stress and experience the rewards of your profession.

Task 1: Skimming.

Decide whether the following statements are true(T) or false(F) after skimming the passage.

1. In order to improve your job satisfaction, you have to change your thoughts about your job into a positive way.

2. When you find your job is terrible, just stop your thought of doing it.

3. Your perfect performance in your work makes it possible for you to move to another job.

4. "The silver lining" in 4th paragraph means the good aspect in something.

5. In what you're doing every day, you can find at least one thing you're grateful for and enjoy it.

6. The difficult work situations will offer you positive meaning of your work and help you deal with your stress.

Task 2: Scanning.

Scan the passage and complete the following diagram with the sentences given below.

1. Mistakes are something you can learn from.

2. Learn to be grateful for something in your job and try to enjoy it.

3. Having a cheerful outlook on your job is very important.

4. Try to search for the good even in a bad situation.

5. Keep yourself free of having negative attitude to your job.

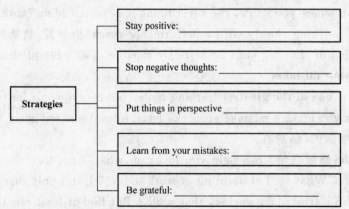

Task 3: Translate the sentences into English.

1. 工作态度的改变不是一朝一夕的事情。

2. 如果有人撞见你在办公室吸烟,你会被罚款的。

3. "全新的思维"能帮助你在逆境中发现好的一面。

4. 感恩的心情能让你关注工作中积极的方面。

5. 积极的心态能帮助你处理好精神压力,体会到职业给你的回报。

Situation Eight (✍ Writing)

Situation: You are working in Zhejiang Huaxin International Trade Co. , Ltd. Your company is interested in importing light industrial products from a trade company in New York. Your manager asks you to write a letter to inquire details about prices and terms of payment.

Zhejiang Huaxin International Trade Co. ,Ltd.

458-410, Hangzhou International Mansion

Hangzhou, China

Jackson Brothers

3487 23rd Street

New York, NY 12009

September 12, 2008

Dear Sirs,

We learn from a friend in New York that you are exporting light industrial products, especially electric appliances. There is a steady demand in our company for the above-mentioned commodities of high quality at moderate prices.

Will you please send us a copy of your catalogue, with details of your prices and terms of payment? We should find it most helpful if you could also supply samples of these goods.

Yours faithfully,

Liu Hua

Task 1: After reading it, you're expected to talk with your partner about how to write inquiries and offers in English.

询盘(Inquiry)

(1)告诉对方通过何种途径得知对方的信息;

(2)介绍本公司情况;

(3)询问对方商品详细情况;

(4)希望对方予以答复。

Useful Phrases and Sentence Patterns

1. inquire/make inquiries about something 询问;询价

2. specifications 规格;明细单

3. delivery date 交货日期

4. be out of stock 没有现货，缺货

5. have in stock 有货

6. goods in stock 现货

7. commission 佣金

8. commission agent 佣金代理人

9. commission house 代办行，佣金行

10. commission merchant 代办商

11. Please see to it that ... 要注意……；务必使……；保证使……

12. We have learned from ... that you are the one producer/dealer/exporter of ....

13. We are glad to inform you that we are the dealer/importer of ... and have engaged/specialized in the line for many years.

14. We are writing to inquire the quotations for ... /we shall be pleased if you send us the lowest quotations for ....

15. Please inform us what special offer you can make/what discount you can make. If you supply goods required，we shall place an order.

16. We are looking forward to your quotations.

报盘(Offer)

(1)感谢对方的询盘；

(2)按对方的要求报盘；

(3)希望对方订货。

Useful Phrases and Sentence Patterns

1. offer 发价，发盘，报盘

2. firm offer 实盘，即不能撤销的发盘。规定了有效期的发价，在该期限内发价人不得予以撤销或变更其内容。

3. non-firm offer 虚盘

4. C&F(Cost and Fright)成本加运费价格(国际贸易通用的价格术语之一)

5. CIF(Cost，Insurance and Fright)成本加保险费及运费

6. terms of payment 付款方式

7. discount 折扣

cash discount 付现折扣

chain discount 连环折扣

quantity discount 数量折扣

trade discount 同业折扣

8. Thank you for your letter/inquiry of (Date)

9. In reply to your letter/inquiry of (Date), we are pleased to quote as follows/we are pleased to make the following offer.

10. We hope these terms are satisfactory and are looking forward to your order.

Task 2: Suppose you are Tommy Steven, a chief buyer of a company. You're writing a letter of inquiry about hand-made gloves in a variety of artificial leathers and ask for catalogues and prices.

Your partner, the sales manager of Kim & Co.,Ltd. has to make an offer according to the Chinese information given below.

(1)发信日期:2009 年 6 月 10 日。

(2)内容:感谢对他们公司生产的人造皮革手套感兴趣,随信附上目录及价目表,并告知公司不仅提供优良服务,而且如果购买数量较大,还可享受折扣。

Self-evaluation

Situation	Standard of Evaluation	Grade			Difficulties and Suggestions
		Excellent	Good	Improved	
Situation 1 Situation 5-6	I can talk about the item freely in a real situation.				
Situation 2-4	I can listen clearly and understand quickly.				
Situation 7	I can get its gist in limited time. I can translate related sentences and the short passage well.				
Situation 8	I can write a practical passage about the inquiry and offer				

Item Thirteen Starting Business

Competence Objectives

1. Students can know some interview tips.
2. Students can talk about a business plan freely in a real situation.
3. Students can know how to do with their career plans.
4. Students can talk about how to become a successful person.
5. Students can talk about how to start their own business.
6. Students can know how to choose right ideas and right business.
7. Students can write a practical passage about the schedule.

Warm-up Activities

After looking through the following pictures, please talk about your future plan after graduation.

Situation One (Discussing)

Situation: Soon you will graduate from your college, congratulations. Maybe you are worried about how to find a good job or how to start your own business. Perhaps you have no idea about your job and your own business in society. Take it easy. First, let us watch the video show which will give some new ideas.

Task: After watching the show—How to prepare for starting your business, please discuss the following questions.

1. What does the man talk about?

_____

2. Can you talk about some starting business tips?

_____

3. Do you want to start your own business or find a good job? Why?

Situation Two (Listening)

Situation: Susan is opening a new company. She has just hired Helen Parker as the company's marketing manager. Today, they are discussing business plans.

Task: **Listen to the conversation. Match the information in Column A with that in Column B according to the conversation. The conversation will be spoken twice.**

Column A (Name)   Column B(Suggestions)
Susan   a. moving in any time after July first
Helen   b. wanting to read the marketing plan
The art people   c. helping out with purchasing new equipment
                                d. investigating factories
                                e. calling to discuss the design of our logos

Situation Three (Listening)

Situation: Several months later, Xiao Wang will leave his college to hunt a job or be self-employed. He doesn't know his goal clearly. And he doesn't know what will happen in the future, either. His close friend advises him to listen to a professor's speech on Monday, so he comes to the 2nd lecture hall to listen to the professor's lecture.

Task: **You will hear one passage of the speech, but with some words or phrases missing. The passage will be read twice. After the second reading, you are required to put the missing words or phrases. Now the passage will begin.**

How should we know what we really want to do? Between our dream and _____, there are too many different _____. If you work hard, you may get your goal, but a dream doesn't always come true. We must know our goals clearly, do what we want, and study harder than before, to get ready for every _____ the god has given us. Everyone needs _____ development. I believe that life is like the weather: we can't know what will happen next; maybe it will rain or be a sunny day, or even it might _____, but we can do something for ourselves, we can make plans for our future to let our future more successful.

Situation Four (Listening)

Situation: Everyone has a career goal, but how to make it come true is still a problem for college students. Your classmate will talk about her career planning. Maybe what she has said will give you some help about it.

Task: **Listen to what she has said and answer the following questions. The passage** will be spoken twice. **Before you listen, learn the following words and expressions.**

Words & Expressions	
accompany 陪伴,伴奏	pluralism talent 复合人才
adapt to 适合	characteristic 特性,特征

1. What is your classmate busy with at present?

_____

2. What is your classmate's career goal?

_____

3. How does your classmate face the reality?

_____

Situation Five (◡Speaking)

Situation: Everyone wants to have his own successful career. And what kind of
person is successful in his career? How to become a successful person
in your career? Different people have different ideas.

**Task:Now discuss with your classmates and report them in class. The following
words and phrases will help you.**

1. One person's characters: competitive, confident, curious, careful, humorous, brave, open-minded, optimistic, honest, hard-working, persistent.

2. Successful factors: inspiration, talent, great effort, money, time, power,
love, higher education, choosing the right business, understanding from others,
good health, many true friends, a nice family, great achievements in one's fields.

Situation Six (◡Speaking)

Situation: You will graduate from our college and begin your own career.
Facing the present financial crisis, it's more challenging for you to
find a desirable job in society. Maybe some of you want to start
your own business. But you have no idea how to start a small business.

**Task:Now discuss the situation with your classmates, and then present your ideas
in front of the class. The following passages will help you.**

Situation Seven (◡Reading)

Situation: Everyone wants to have his own ideas about business. The students are inquiring an expert to give them some recommendations for their investment.

Task：**Read the passage to get the idea about what the expert has recommended and then finish the tasks.**

Pursue Success with an Idea That Excites You and Customers Alike

Every successful business starts with a great idea, but not all great ideas result in a successful business. So how do successful **entrepreneurs**（企业家）catch the right idea in a stream of clever business **schemes**（计划）? With patience. When you take the time to properly develop your ideas, the result.is a business that **simultaneously**（同时地）：(1) Inspires you. (2)Makes you happy. (3)Meets your customers' needs.

Know yourself

Capitalize（利用）on your own experience — whether you're a **veteran**（富有经验的人）in a specific industry or a simple **hobbyist**（沉溺于某种癖好者）with boundless knowledge — to create good ideas with great **odds**（可能的机会）. But before deciding what business is best for you, you must decide if you're ready to do the hard work to make it happen.

I recommend：Discover if you've got what it takes to be a successful entrepreneur by taking self-employment **quizzes**（测试）.

Do what you love to do

You must be passionate about your ideas in order to make them fly; if you're not, they'll **flounder**（困难地往前走）. Think about the things that make you happy：Is there a business idea there?

I recommend：Discover which of your passions will mix well with your personality in order to create a successful business which helps budding entrepreneurs identify their natural strengths and talents and match them with a complementary business model.

Do what consumers need do

Supply is useless without demand. Find out what people want and find a way to give it to them.

Do better what someone else already does

The best ideas aren't always new ideas. Examine existing business models that you admire and brainstorm concepts to improve them.

I recommend：Study America's most successful companies for ideas and **inspiration**（灵感）. The *Fortune* 500 list ranks the nation's largest corporations — many of which used to be small, just like you.

Do what's been proven successful to do

If you're a new business owner, consider purchasing a **franchise**(特许经营权). The best business for you might end up(结束)being one that a **franchisor**(授予特许者) has already spent millions of dollars to develop, test and grow.

Tips & Tactics
Helpful advice for making the most of this Guide

Consider all your ideas — and those of friends and family — carefully. Don't dismiss suggestions too quickly; your best idea might be your least likely one.

Many entrepreneurs consider themselves **jacks of all trades**(万事通); most businesses, by contrast, must be highly focused to succeed. Find a **niche**(合适的领域) and be an expert rather than a **generalist**(通才).

The right business for you will be in an industry and a market where there is room for you; avoid pursuing a business that is already **saturated with**(使饱和) competition.

Whatever business you choose, you'll have to make a living doing it. Be **realistic**(现实的), then, about whether you'll be happy doing it, and whether consumers will actually pay you for it.

Task 1: Getting a message.

After reading the passage, decide whether the following statements are true (T) or false(F).

1. All great ideas result in a successful business.

2. But before deciding what business is best for you, you must know yourself.

3. Supply is useless without demand.

4. The best ideas are always new ideas.

5. You may not be passionate about your ideas in order to make them fly.

6. Whatever business you choose, you'll have to make a living doing it.

Task 2: Skimming and scanning.

Scan the passage and answer the following questions.

1. What kind of business is the right business?

_____

2. According to the passage, can you tell us some tips about how to choose the right business and the idea?

_____

Task 3: Translate the sentences into English.

1. 为了让你放飞梦想,你对自己的点子一定要有激情。

2. 如果你不能适应社会的要求,你一定会被社会淘汰。

3. 职业规划包括收集自己和行业方面的信息,估计行动过程可能的结果,最后选择我们觉得有吸引力、切实可行的事情。

4. 每个成功的事业都开始于一个好点子,但并不是所有的好点子都导致一份成功的事业。

5. 对你来说,正确的生意就是处在还有生存空间的行业和市场。

Situation Eight (✒ Writing)

Situation: You have successfully started your own company. You want to hire a new secretary, so you ask one candidate to read the following conference schedule.

Conference Schedule

Dec. 20, 2008

8:30—9:00	Registration
9:10—9:30	Introduction of VIPs by moderator(主持人)
9:40—10:35	Negotiation of two companies
10:40—11:40	A report by an expert from ABC company
11:50—13:30	Lunch and break
13:50—14:50	To review the progress of internet industry
15:00—15:30	Coffee break
15:35—16:30	Visiting Jiangsu Software Industry Base
16:40—17:30	Group discussion after visiting
17:40—18:30	Closing speech
18:40	Dinner party

Jiangsu Bureau of Science and Technology

Task 1: After reading it, firstly you expect the candidate to talk about his ideas about how to write a schedule and understand his basic writing skills.

日程表

日程表常采用表格的形式把会议的时间和事情安排列出。它通常包括日程的名称、制定日程表的时间、主要内容安排列表、制定日程表的单位或个人的名称、注意事项等内容。其语言通常使用祈使句、省略句、不完整句,多使用名词词组。

Useful Phrases and Sentence Patterns

registration 注册

pick up 接人

check in 登记,报到

opening ceremony 开幕仪式

welcome and opening address by ...   由……致欢迎词

check out 结账

under auspices of ...   由……单位主办

Task 2: After some guests having visited your company, you ask your secretary to make a schedule for your guests to arrange a tour to your hometown, Nanjing. Complete the schedule for some guests to visit your hometown in English.

	Schedule
Saturday Nov. 18	7:30 _____ (在宾馆大厅集合) 7:45 Take coach to Zhongshan Museum 11:10—11:40 _____ (乘车游览市区) 12:00 _____ (在宾馆吃午餐) 14:00 Take coach to Lingyin Temple 17:30 _____ (晚宴)
Sunday Nov. 19	8:30 Take coach to Confucian Temple 11:30 Have lunch at one restaurant 14:00 _____ (前往市中心购物) 17:00 Dinner at Nanjing Restaurant 19:00 _____ (去火车站)

Self-evaluation

Situation	Standard of Evaluation	Grade			Difficulties and Suggestions
		Excellent	Good	Improved	
Situation 1 Situation 5-6	I can talk about the item freely in a real situation.				
Situation 2-4	I can listen clearly and understand quickly.				
Situation 7	I can get its gist in limited time. I can translate related sentences and the short passage well.				
Situation 8	I can write a practical passage about the schedule.				

Item Fourteen   Dealing with Money

Competence Objectives

1. Students can know different ways of dealing with money.
2. Students can know how to deposit money with/in a bank.
3. Students can know how to buy and sell shares.
4. Students can know what an insurance is.
5. Students can know how to withdraw money with/from a bank.
6. Students can know how to diversify portfolio.
7. Students can write a memo.

Warm-up Activities

Are you familiar with the following currencies?

Situation One (Discussing)

Situation: At the end of the year, your father and mother intend to deal with their spare money, and your uncle who majors in investment is giving his suggestions to them by reading the following pictures. Do you know what the following pictures stand for?

Task: What roles do they play in your daily life, especially when you have spare money? Talk with your partner please. The following patterns or words are for reference.

CHINA LIFE
中国人寿

人民币存款利率表
日期: 2007-12-21

项目	年利率%
一、城乡居民及单位存款	
（一）活期	0.72
（二）定期	
1.整存整取	
三个月	3.33
半年	3.78
一年	4.14
二年	4.68
三年	5.4
五年	5.85
2.零存整取、整存零取、存本取息	
一年	3.33
三年	3.78
五年	4.14
3.定活两便	按一年以内定期整存整取同档次利率打6折
二、协定存款	1.53
三、通知存款	
一天	1.17
七天	1.71

注：人民银行历次存款利息调整明细表

Patterns or words for reference

1. We prefer depositing money in a bank.

2. I'd like to set aside some money for my children's education.

3. I don't think investing in housing is advisable.

4. Would you make some recommendations to us?

5. Chinese like saving money for emergency.

6. There is a high risk as well as a high income.

7. Real estate investment is a high-risk, high-income investment.

8. What can we benefit from ...

9. Life insurance is unique among financial instruments.

10. You have to pay an insurance company what are called premiums.

11. Life can be divided into risk protection of life insurance and finance and investment-type life insurance.

12. Would you please introduce stock exchange to us?

13. How do I buy and sell stocks?

Situation Two (Listening)

Situation: My friend Tom has just got his pay for his part-time job. Now he is entering a bank to deposit it.

Task: After listening to the dialogue twice, you are required to tell others how to deposit money in the bank.

Words & Expressions

Business Department of ICBC	中国工商银行营业部
fixed deposit or current deposit	定期或活期存款
current	流通的，现在的
deposit	存款，定金
fill out a deposit slip	填写存款单
account	账户
account number and amount	账号和数量
passbook	银行存折
input your secret code	输入密码
check slip	对账单

Situation Three (Listening)

Situation: Miss Green is browsing the share-list.

Task: **After listening to the dialogue twice, you are expected to tell others what business Miss Green wants to do.**

Words & Expressions

asking price of the stock	股票报价
share	股，股票

Situation Four （Listening）

Situation： An insurance agent came into your home to do promotion.

Task：Please listen to his explanation and then tell your parents when the insurance company will pay the policyholder and how they will do.

Words & Expressions			
written agreement	书面协议	pay for losses	赔付损失
policy	保单	premium	保险费
policyholder	投保人		

Situation Five （Speaking）

Situation： Since you plan to take a training class for CET6, you step into a bank to withdraw 300 Yuan.

Task：Make a dialogue with your partner who acts as a bank clerk with the help of the following patterns.

1. I want to withdraw some money from my All-In-One passbook.
   我想从"活期一本通"存折上取一些钱。

2. Fill out a withdrawal slip.
   填写取款凭条。

3. Will you please give me your passbook with the slip?

请把存折和取款单给我好吗？

4. How much do you want?

你取多少？

5. How do you want the money?

你要什么样的票面？

6. Thirty tens and twenty fives please, and the rest as you would like.

三十张十元币，二十张五元币，其他随意。

7. Enter your secret code.

请输入密码。

8. Here is the money with your interest note.

请收好钱及利息单。

Situation Six (⬭Reading)

Situation: As the economy crisis is getting to every corner, more and more people are concerned about the safety of their savings. They are inquiring an expert to give them some recommendations for their investment.

Task: Read the passage to get the idea about what the expert recommends and then finish the tasks.

Vary Your Investment

How to reduce the risk of investment? Spreading your money among many different kinds of investments, such as stocks, bonds, and short-term investments may be a good way. Various investments tend to provide less **volatile**(不稳定的) returns over the long term and can help **minimize**(减到最少) downward risk. Therefore, you are less likely to be affected by the performance of one single investment.

If you want to know the details, you may refer to the following information.

Stocks provide the opportunity for higher growth over the long-term. But this greater **potential**(潜在的) reward carries a greater risk, particularly in the short-term, because market changes may mean your investment is worth less when you sell it.

Bonds(债券) provide regular income and lower risk, by contrast with the stock market which is unpredictable ups and downs. Often, bonds do not move in the same direction as stocks. Investors who are more concerned about safety rather than growth often prefer holding government or insured bond investments rather than stocks.

Short-term investments include money market funds and short-term **deposit**(存款). Money market funds provide you easy access to your money. They are considered **conservative**(保守的) investments and offer **stability**(稳定) of **principal**(本金), but they usually have lower returns compared to bond funds or individual bonds.

How to plan your investment then? It will depend on your investment goals.

In general, the first aspect you should take into consideration is the amount of time you have until you need the money you are investing.

For an investor who has a longer time free of money and is willing to take on additional risk in pursuit of long-term growth, a larger percentage in stocks may be appropriate.

As you get closer to your goal, you may want to shift your investments into more conservative **securities**(有价证券), such as **Treasury Bonds**(国库券).

In retirement, a good portion of your money should be in stable investments, but you should also continue to invest to fight with **inflation**(通货膨胀).

Regardless of what kind of investment you choose, a varied investment can help ensure success in meeting your future goals. A well thought-out plan is the key: your money is too important to invest without a plan.

Task 1: Getting a message.

After reading the passage, decide whether the following statements are true (T) or false(F)

1. Varying your investment can help minimize downward risk.

2. Stock market is stable.

3. Bonds may offer you higher growth with lower risk.

4. Short-term investments offer you lower returns but more stable.

5. If you can keep a large amount of money for quite several years, it is better for you to invest in stocks.

Task 2: Skimming and scanning.

Choose one topic from the followings to talk with your partner.

1. What do you know about investment?

2. What way do you prefer to invest if you have a large sum of money?

3. What can you infer from the last but one paragraph?

Task 3: Translate the sentences into English.

1. 你要活期储蓄还是定期储蓄?

2. 不顾风险投资是不理智的。

3. 深思熟虑的计划能为你的投资收益带来保证。

4. 那些更关注安全而不是增长的投资者喜欢储蓄。

5. 采用多种投资组合的投资者会承担较小的风险。

Situation Seven (☞ Writing)

Situation：You have just applied for a job as a secretary. Now you are reading a
memo.

Memo

To：All staff

From：Mr. Lawson, personnel manager

Date ：Sept. 26，2008

Subject：Business hours change

After much discussion, it is agreed that we'll change our business hours on
the coming golden holiday. The starting hour will be half an hour earlier than
usual, that is 8：00 A. M. , and the ending hour is one hour later that is 10 P.
M. .

This change will take effect from Sept. 30 till Oct. 8.

**Task 1：After reading it, firstly you are expected to exchange your ideas about how
to write a memo with your predecessor before reading the following reference.**

备忘录(Memo) 与电话记录(Telephone message)

备忘录是一种非正式公文。它是在本单位内部为了联系工作,分管某项工作的
有关人员或是下级部门所使用的一种简短书面交流形式。备忘录的主要目的是针对
某一事情提醒、督促、通告本单位内部的相关人员。备忘录的书写格式如下。

Memorandum 或 Memo：写在信笺的最上端正中。

To(收件人)：在 To 的后面写收件人的姓名,或者职务,可免写称谓。

From(发件人)：在 From 的后面写发件人的姓名,一般情况下免写职务,免写称
谓。

Date：写在信笺的右上角或左边齐头。

Subject/Re：用几个字对备忘录内容进行概括,要求简洁。

Body：备忘录可免称呼,客套用语. 语言简洁明了,篇幅短小精悍,常用非正式用
语。如果呈送领导,措辞可以正式一些。

另外,附件(attachment)、副本抄送标志(C：copy, CC：carbon copy, PC：pho-
tocopy)和附言(postscript)可酌情删减。

Reference Initials (经手人代号)：撰写人姓名首字母。

电话记录的形式类同备忘录,只是时间需要详细到小时甚至分钟。

Task 2: John Brown is waiting for you to help him to write a memo according to the given information.

至:采购部经理

自:布朗·约翰

事由:电脑

我们办公室急需一台电脑,以便方便与外国公司联系,9 月 8 号的经理会议已经同意,请您尽早解决。

时间:2008 年 9 月 20 日。

Self-evaluation

Situation	Standard of Evaluation	Grade			Difficulties and Suggestions
		Excellent	Good	Improved	
Situation 1 Situation 5	I can talk about the item freely in a real situation.				
Situation 2-4	I can listen clearly and understand quickly.				
Situation 6	I can get its gist in limited time. I can translate related sentences and the short passage well.				
Situation 7	I can write a practical passage about the memo.				

Item Fifteen　Friendship, Families and Love

Competence Objectives

1. Students can know what love is.
2. Students can tell the differences between love and marriages.
3. Students can know the responsibility of being a husband or a wife.
4. Students will respect their parents better.
5. Students can know how to deal with friendship and love.
6. Students can know which is more important to study or to love in college.
7. Students can write an apology letter.

Warm-up Activities

After looking through the following pictures, please talk about the subject on friendship, love and marriage.

Situation One (Discussing)

Situation: Mr. James is having an English lesson. The students in his class are debating on a topic, "Is romantic love the most important condition for marriage?"

Task: **Please fill in the following blanks according to the examples on the above debate.**

	Arguments	Counter-arguments
1	Marriage is the result and extension of love. Therefore, romantic love is the most important condition for marriage.	A marriage based on romantic love alone will not last long, for a sense of responsibility is most essential to a successful marriage.
2	Love should be the most important condition for marriage because a marriage without love is like hell in which the couple suffer for the rest of their lives.	Love is not the most important condition for marriage because love is romantic whereas marriage is practical.

续

	Arguments	Counter-arguments
3		
4		
5		
6		
7		
8		
9		
10		

Situation Two (Listening)

Situation: Wang Qian and Zhang Lin are talking about their families and marriages.

Task: After listening to the dialogue twice, you are required to tell others how to understand a single-child policy in China.

Situation Three (Listening)

Situation: Lucy's wedding is going to be held in three weeks.

Task: After listening to the dialogue twice, you are expected to tell others what she wants to prepare for it.

Situation Four (Listening)

Situation: Marriage is a basic and important part of human life. Successful marriage is the most effective form of social support. It relieves the effects of stress, and leads to better mental and physical health.

Task: After listening to the material twice, you are expected to tell others your opinion about marriage.

Situation Five (Speaking)

Situation: You have no true understanding of friendship and love. Your friend asks you to read a poet. This will help you.

Task: Read the following poet and say something about your understanding on friendship and love.

Friendship and Love

Friendship is a quiet walk in the park with the one you trust.

Love is when you feel like you are the two around.

Friendship is when they gaze into your eyes and you know they care.

Love is when they gaze into your eyes and it warms your heart.

Friendship is being close even when you are apart.

Love is you can still feel their hand on your heart when they are not near.

Friendship is hoping that they experience the very best.

Love is when you bring them the very best.

Friendship occupies your mind, love occupies your soul.

Friendship is knowing that you will always try to be there when in need.

Love is a warming touch that sends a pulse through your heart.

Friendship can survive without love.

Love cannot live without friendship.

Situation Six (Reading)

Situation: Marriages based on love tend to create a happy and harmonious atmosphere in the family which is good for the development of children.

Task: Read the passage to get the idea and then finish the tasks.

Love and Marriage

It was a fine day in spring. Everything was coming back to life, but a marriage was ending in the office of residents' committee. It was a very old couple. The man, Robert Linton, was ninety-four years old, and the woman, Emily Waller, was ninety years old. It was hard to believe that they were getting divorced after they had been married for more than seventy years. A middle-aged woman, Susan, tried her best to persuade them not to divorce, but they refused. They had waited for the day for about fifty years. No one could change their minds, except their children. But the last of their children had passed away a month ago.

"Why do you insist on divorce? Don't you have another way to solve your problems?" Susan asked.

Robert said, "No. We decided this many years ago, and both of us kept our promise to wait. Now, it is the time for fulfill the promise."

"What is your promise?"

"We promised that we would not divorce until our children all passed away." Emily answered, "We loved them and hoped all of them would be happy. They were our responsibilities. We had to do everything which is good for them."

"Do you love each other now?" Susan asked again.

Robert shot a glance at Emily, and smiled. After a moment, he said, "Yes, I loved her very much. That's why she married me."

"No," Emily interrupted him, "I married you just because my mother thought you were a talented person. She believed you could give me a better life than the other people who proposed to me."

"Maybe. I fell in love with you when I was sixteen. You were my first lover, and also the last. I didn't know how to show you my love because of your beauty. The only thing I could do was to accompany you, no matter what happened, no matter what you did, and no matter what time it was. I could only stay beside you."

"In fact, that was the very reason why I chose you." Emily said, "I knew I had to marry someone, because I had reached the age of marriage. The others only loved my beauty, but you, you were the most special one. Your family was not rich at that time, and you had many brothers and sisters. But you were kind and, most importantly I believed that you loved who I really was."

Robert gazed at Emily for a few minutes and then continued, "When you agreed to marry me, I couldn't believe my ears. You were so splendid and I was so plain. When you smiled at me, at that moment, it seemed that the sun had appeared in front of me. I was the happiest person in the world when I held your hands."

"I know. The first time you held my hand, you were so nervous that your hands were sweating. At that moment, I knew you really loved me and I told myself you were my Mr. Right. No matter what others thought, I would marry you. I believed you could take care of me all your life."

"When you were pregnant, I looked like an idiot. When I went to work, I was worried about you. I was afraid you might be hurt. I felt anxious every minute, and always imagined what were doing. After work, I flew back to look after you. I loved you, so I did not care that the other men said I was too scared for you."

"I love you, too."

They were holding their hands and gazed at each other.

"Then, if you love each other, why do you stick to divorce?" Susan inserted.

"Time changed everything." Emily said as they relaxed their grip, "After the birth of Jack, we always quarreled because of the child and our housework. Two years later, our first daughter was born. We were all busy with our work. After a full day's work, we were all tired and had no energy to do anything. But, we had to look after our children and do all the housework. We did not have enough money to employ a person to do these things, so we had to depend on ourselves. We were all bored of doing those trifles, so we quarreled again and again and again. We couldn't help hurting each other, even hurting our children. At last, we realized we needed to have a talk because our children were deeply hurt. We were not lovers by then, but we were parents. Our children had to have good surroundings to grow up in, so we kept our anger hidden and let them out in other ways. Then we had another girl and another boy."

"I do not love him now, but I love my children."

"Me, too. So we decided not to divorce unless all our children died. Now, they have all passed away, and we can make our promise come true. The first half of our life was for our children, but now, it belongs to us."

"Do you hate each other?"

"Hate? No." Emily smiled, "We are too old to hate anybody, especially the person who has lived with you for more than seventy years."

"Child, have you heard that hate is coming from love? Now, we do not love each other, so we do not hate anymore." Robert laughed.

Outside, it was a nice spring day.

Three months later, Robert died of heart disease, and two weeks later, Emily died in her bed peacefully.

Task 1: Skimming.

After reading the passage, decide whether the following statements are true (T) or false(F).

1. Robert Linton and Emily got divorced after they had been married for more than seventy years.

2. They decided that they would divorce many years ago.

3. Robert Linton and Emily hated each other.

4. When Emily agreed to marry Robert Linton, he couldn't believe his ears.

5. Robert Linton and Emily loved each other when they married.

Task 2: Discussion.

Choose one topic from the followings to discuss with your partner.

1. How do you understand love and marriage?

2. Do you agree with this sentence "marriage is responsibility"?

3. Great marriage in my heart.

Task 3: Translate the sentences into English.

1. 婚姻是爱情的结果和延伸。

2. 我们的孩子必须有好的成长环境。

3. 成功的婚姻是维系社会的最有效的形式。

4. 当凯瑟琳怀孕时,她看上去就像一个球。

5. 在我的第一个孩子出生后,我们总是因为孩子和家务争吵。

Situation Seven (✒ Writing)

Situation 1: Jane was very happy to receive beautiful flowers from her friend Laura. Now you are going to read her thank-you letter.

Dear Laura,

I was truly enraptured beyond expression to receive your flowers which turned our living room into a garden. How considerate and wonderful of you to remember my birthday! You just couldn't have selected anything I had liked more! You have a positive genius for selecting the right gift!

The four years I spent with you at the college have been the pleasantest period in my life. I will cherish this memory forever. How nice it would be to see you again.

You have been more than kind, and I won't ever forget it. My love and deepest gratitude, now and always!

Sincerely yours,

Jane

Situation 2: Harris failed to meet Mr. David according to their engagement. Please read his apology letter to Mr. David.

Dear Mr. David,

Much to my regret I was unable to keep my engagement to meet you at the park gate. I fear you are displeased at my failing to keep my promise, but I trust you will forgive me. Let me explain. My mother suddenly fell sick early yesterday morning, and I had to send her to hospital.

I shall be obliged if you will kindly write and tell me when and where we may meet again. I hope to see you soon.

Your sincerely,

Harris

Task 1：After reading them, firstly you are expected to exchange your ideas about how to write a thank-you letter and an apology letter with your predecessor before reading the following reference.

感谢信

人们在交往中常需要相互致谢,收到别人赠送的礼物,得到别人的帮助,受到别人的慰问,都应该表示感谢。感谢信是人们常用的一种感谢方式。

感谢信最主要的特点是真诚。缺乏真挚的感情答谢他人,收信人将对你的谢意产生怀疑,感谢的目的也就失去了。因此,写感谢信首先得真心诚意。

感谢信另一个特点是具体。写感谢信切忌泛泛而谈,而应该着重于具体的感谢事由。

感谢信还有一个特点是及时。收到别人礼物、得到别人帮助,应及时写信予以答谢。否则,人家会对你的谢意大打折扣。

收到他人赠送的礼物应当及时写封感谢信,感谢信除了应写得真诚、具体、及时外,还应当特别提及所收礼物的具体内容,否则,泛泛而谈,使人觉得你不够真诚。为此,当你写感谢信时,应这样写:"Thank you for your beautiful roses"(谢谢您送的美丽的玫瑰花);而不要笼统地写上"Thank you for your beautiful gift"(谢谢您送给我的漂亮礼物),这样,使人觉得你既礼貌,又诚心,从而真正达到交往的目的。

道歉信

日常生活中难免会出现一些差错,如失约、损坏东西等。遇到这种情形,应及时写信致歉,以消除不必要的误解,维系正常的关系。道歉信除应及时写之外,还必须写得诚恳,歉意应发自内心,决不可敷衍塞责。再则,事情原委要解释清楚,措辞应当委婉贴切。写好道歉信的关键在于措辞要朴实委婉,语气要诚恳真挚,解释要详细明了。如"much to my regret","I'm excessively sorry","a feeling of deep regret"都是致歉之词,用上这些词能恰如其分地表达了写信人的真诚歉意。

Task 2：

1. Jim and Mary are waiting for you to help them to write a thank-you letter ac-

cording to the given information.

Dan 和 Laura 送一对漂亮的花瓶给 Jim 和 Mary 作为新婚礼物,他们新婚夫妇很感激,且觉得这个礼物用心周到、可爱又实用,他们准备将花瓶装饰在房间里,并准备在婚礼后与他们聚一聚。

2. **Russell is waiting for you to help him to write an apology letter according to the given information.**

彼得想从拉塞尔那里借字典,拉塞尔正在用此字典,他答应给他买一本,但没买到。拉塞尔为不能给彼得提供帮助而深感歉意。

Self-evaluation

Situation	Standard of Evaluation	Grade			Difficulties and Suggestions
		Excellent	Good	Improved	
Situation 1 Situation 5	I can talk about the item freely in a real situation.				
Situation 2-4	I can listen clearly and understand quickly.				
Situation 6	I can get its gist in limited time. I can translate related sentences and the short passage well.				
Situation 7	I can write a practical passage about thank-you letters and apology letters.				

Keys for Reference

Keys to Item One

Situation One

1. Open-ended.
2. Convenient, exciting, useful, popular ...
3. Making a telephone call, writing a letter, chatting online, e-mailing, sending a message, talking face to face ...

Situation Two

1. In the meeting room.
2. Johnson.
3. At IBM, in the International section.

Situation Three

1. breakfast   2. Tower   3. Science   4. tallest   5. sights

Situation Four

1. She was a secretary in an American company.
2. She came from Canada.
3. Because she shared it with two other people.
4. They usually see each other or talk on the telephone over the weekends.
5. Caddy seemed to be getting impatient. She started going out by herself at lunch time instead of eating with Fang, and she seemed unwilling to answer questions.

Situation Five

Situation 1: **Phone to a tourist agency for a trip to Suzhou.**

A: Hello, this is Edward Freda. Can I talk to Miss Zhao?

B: She is not here but you can contact her by cell phone or would you like to try again an hour later?

A: Thank you, by the way, could you please tell me something about the trip to Suzhou?

B: I'm sorry, I'm her friend Xiao Wang, I know nothing about it.

A: I'll ring back later, thanks all the same.

Situation 2: Phone to your friend for planning the weekend activities.

Jackson: Hello! This is Jackson speaking. May I speak to Tom, please?

Tom: Hi, Jackson.

Jackson: Are you busy this weekend? What are you going to do this weekend?

Tom: I'm free this weekend. I have no plan. How about you?

Jackson: I'm free too, if the weather is fine, shall we play football with our classmates?

Tom: It's wonderful. When and where shall we meet?

Jackson: Let's meet at the west gate of our college at 8:00 on Saturday morning.

Tom: That's OK. See you then.

Jackson: See you.

Situation Six

Task 1

1. T 2. F 3. T 4. F 5. F

6. T 7. T 8. T 9. F 10. T

Task 2

1. Communication — such a vital part of keeping marriages healthy! The greatest of problems can be solved with good communication. Even the smallest of problems can be insurmountable without it!

2. The world we are living in is amazing. There are countless living things. How can they live harmoniously? The answer is also communication.

Task 3

1. Speaking through eyes is more effective.

2. A look at the audience and a pause before speech help to create a good impression on the audience.

3. Throughout the speech you should keep eye contact with the audience.

4. If you just talk without eye contact with the audience, they will feel that they are being ignored and it is quite likely that they also have no interests in whatever you're trying to convey.

5. As human beings we should communicate with each other to make the earth peaceful.

Situation Seven

Task 2

1.

Dear Robert,

With sincere wishes for your health and happiness.

Yours truly,

Bill

2.

Haihe Scientific and Technological

Development Co. ,Ltd.

Zhou Baoshan

Deputy General Manager

Add: P. O. Box 15   Tel:3890760(O)

Lane 3, Wenhua Road   3914387(H)

Heping District   Fax: (011) 3890434

Haihe, P. R. China   Mobile: 13335478685

Zip:114709

Keys to Item Two

Warm-up Activities

boiled dumplings / French fries / chicken wings / steamed buns/
ice cream / coca-cola / maize / juice / salad / rice dumpling /
pork braised in brown sauce / moon cake

Situation One

Open-ended.

Situation Two

1. They are going to go for a picnic.
2. It's a fine day.
3. In an hour and a half.
4. Nancy and Jim.

Situation Three

1. Cookies.

2. Chocolate, and almond-flavored.

3. No, it's really quite easy.

Situation Four

(1) Fast food offers a most efficient way to eat.

(2) Fast food restaurants provide us with a good environment for entertainment and study.

(3) Youngsters can even find good opportunities of working practice in some fast food restaurants.

Situation Five

Dialogue (1)

A: Are you ready to order now, sir?

B: Yes. I'd like to have tomato soup, roast beef, and mashed potatoes.

A: How do you want the beef? Rare, medium or well-done?

B: Well-done, please.

A: Anything to drink?

B: Water will be fine.

Dialogue (2)

A: What kind of Chinese food would you like to have, Mr. Hill?

B: Mr. Gao, I really don't know. Why not order for me?

A: OK. How about trying Mongolian Barbecue? It's different from what you had before.

B: Fine. Whatever you say.

A: How do you want your beef?

B: Medium rare, please.

Dialogue (3)

A: May I help you?

B: Yes. I'd like to order ham and eggs, please.

A: How do you want your eggs?

B: Scrambled, please.

A: Anything else?

B: One orange juice. Make it small.

Situation Six

Great changes have taken place in Chinese people's diet in the past five years.

The proportion of grain, which is the main food for Chinese people, has decreased by 4% from 1986 to 1990. Meanwhile, the proportion of milk has constantly increased. The reasons why Chinese people's food preference changes are as follows: firstly, the income of urban and rural residents has been constantly increased owing to the economic reforms. People have great consuming capacity on their diet. Secondly, the global markets provide diverse choices for Chinese people. Thirdly, Chinese's attitude towards food is changing. People have gradually realized the importance of a balanced and healthy diet.

Situation Seven

Task 1

1. C   2. B   3. C   4. D   5. A

Task 2

1. Nowadays, with the improvement of people's living standards, health is a hot topic that many people are concerned about. But how to keep healthy? In my opinion, appropriate and healthy food is the key part in keeping healthy. Every day, we eat a variety of food in order to keep our body in balance. Our body needs various food which offer different nutrients. But too much chocolate and ice-cream may get us fat or even sick. So we must be careful about what we eat and how much we eat. In a word, reasonable and balanced diets are the keys to staying healthy. So we should pay more attention to healthy food.

2. As we know, health is more important than wealth. Food gives us energy, so we must have enough food to keep healthy. We should eat more fruit and vegetables but less meat, and we must also have right kinds of food. A cup of milk a day can help make us healthy as well. Different food help us in different ways, if we eat too little or too much, or if we choose the wrong food, we may become sick, so we must have meals three times a day on time, too. It's necessary for us to have healthy eating habits.

3. People's health is affected greatly by what they eat. In Scotland, eating habits are the second major cause, after smoking, of poor health. The national diet contributes to a range of serious illnesses which include coronary heart disease, certain cancers, strokes, osteoporosis, and diabetes.

Task 3

1. Science has made enormous steps in the past five years.

2. Forty percent of cancer is indirectly related to the diet.

3. Food additives are harmful to health.

4. The nurse injected penicillin into her arm.

5. The farmers are trying to fatten the animals in order to obtain a higher price.

Situation Eight

Task 1

When Westerners wish to invite people to dinner, it is necessary to extend the invitation a week or so in advance(约提前一周发请柬) as people may have other plans. The invitation may be given directly or over the phone. If the occasion is very formal, a letter or an invitation card needs to be sent. In this case the invitee should reply so that the host will know whether he can come or not.

Most spoken invitations are in the form of questions. If a guest accepts the invitation, he or she should express his or her pleasure or thanks. If a guest declines (拒绝), he or she should speak with grace and courtesy (谦恭，礼貌). Some explanation should be given. For formal invitations, printed cards are sent. The following are the examples.

Task 2

Dear Harry,

　　It's very kind of you and Margaret to invite us to dinner this coming Saturday evening. We thank you and are delighted to accept ... /but to our regrets, we cannot make it.

Yours sincerely,

John

Keys to Item Three

Situation One

Task 1

Tian'anmen Square (the Gate of Heavenly Peace)/Sanya/West Lake/the Yellow Crane Tower/Huangshan Mountain/Shanghai Oriental Pearl Tower

Task 2

Huangshan Mountain (Yellow Mountain) is the name of the 72 peaks range lying in the south of Anhui province which has been designated as a national park and declared as a World Natural and Cultural Heritage area by UNESCO. There is a famous saying in

China "The landscape of the Five Famous Mountains tops/belittles those else-where, and the landscape of Huangshan Mountain tops/belittles that of the Five Fa-mous Mountains." The ancient pines, bizarre rocks, the seas of cloud, unique granite peaks, etc. attract billions of tourists throughout the world. So if I have a chance to go out for a traveling, I prefer to go to Huangshan (Yellow Mountain).

Situation Two

1. He will fly back to London.
2. He has to to pay RMB 1,400 yuan.
3. The airplane will take off at 9:30 in the morning.

Situation Three

Task 1
1. T 2. F 3. F 4. T 5. F 6. F

Task 2
1. Wuhan   2. summer vacation   3. fantastic
4. friendly   5. delicious and cheap   6. hot/horrible
7. interesting places   8. scenic spot

Situation Four

1. B 2. D 3. D 4. C

Situation Five

Task 1
(1) Prepare the luggage.

If you plan to go out for a trip, list all things on a piece of paper. If you wish to visit Hainan in summer, don't forget your summer wear, because it's very hot there. If you will go to Huangshan, take your raincoat. And don't forget to take your digital camera.

(2) Take necessary medicines.

It is a good habit to take some necessary medicines when traveling. Who can be sure that he will not fall sick when visiting attractions?

(3) Get some information about the local customs.

As a saying goes, "Do as the Romans do". It is advisable to learn some cus-toms.

(4) Choose a good travel agency.

A famous agency may cost you more, but may provide you with better service, better tour guide and better hotels.

(5)Don't bring too much cash with you.

It is not safe to bring too much cash when you are traveling. You are suggested to bring your credit cards.

Task 2

A:Do you like traveling?

B:Yes,of course. I often go traveling with my parents.

A:Really? How many places have you visited in China?

B:In China? 15 or 20? I can't remember that.

A:Wow! Cool! Then which city impressed you most?

B:Nanjing, I went there last summer.

A:I heard it is a good place for tourists,there are so many tourist attractions.

B:That's true! I have just been there for 5 days,I just went Ming Tomb,the Mausoleum and Lingu Temple.

A:How is your stay there?

B:Good! It is a beautiful city but it is too hot!

A:I hate that.

B:I don't like hot weather, either. So I'd like to go there in spring next time.

A:Oh, maybe we can go together.

Situation Six

Task 2

People like traveling,visiting new places and learning about different cultures, but traveling means pollution. Tourism is a double-side sword. On one hand,it does good to the development of local economy,affecting society and the environment in many ways. On the other hand,it is destroying the environment gradually. There is no doubt that we can benefit a lot from tourism. We shouldn't prohibit tourism just because it pollutes the environment. The key is keeping tourism from destroying the environment. First we can construct fewer modern facilities at scenic spots than before. Second tourists can be educated about how to protect the environment. I'm sure if we try our best,we can find a balance between tourism and the environment.

Situation Seven

Task 1

1. F 2. T 3. F 4. F 5. F

Task 2

1. Because school is out. Because the weather is great. And most of all, be-

cause we all need a break.

2. For one thing, it's cheaper than traveling abroad, and there's no language problem. But besides that, the vast American territory offers numerous tourist attractions. Major cities offer visitors a variety of urban delights.

3. International business, mass communication and jet airplanes have made the world a global village. People all over the world enjoy going abroad to travel. And no matter where they live, people enjoy visiting scenic spots in their own country. The convenience of modern freeways, railways and airplanes makes travel as easy as pie.

Task 3

1. He journeyed to Paris and other places from time to time.
2. Her sense of humor appealed to him enormously.
3. For one thing, I have no money; for another, I have no time to go traveling.
4. Special protection should be given to the famous national historical sites.
5. I find it necessary to get a map while traveling.

Situation Eight

Task 2

Complaint Letter

Dear Sir or Madame,

　I write this letter to you to make some complaints about the computer I bought in your store yesterday afternoon. There's something wrong with it. That makes me extremely unhappy.

　The computer cannot be properly shut down when I got it back to the office. When I click the shutdown button, it seems that the machine gives no response. And I'm so annoyed with it.

　It's obvious that you didn't carefully examine the machine before you sold it. I think your store should take full responsibility for selling me the defective machine. I insist that you give me a satisfactory reply. I do want you to give back my money as soon as possible.

Sincerely yours,
Tom

Keys to Item Four

Situation One

Open-ended.

Situation Two

Task 1

1. F 2. T 3. F 4. F 5. T

Task 2

1. other than 2. used to like; am interested in 3. How come 4. love

Situation Three

Task 1

Jeff:1,3,4,5,6,9   Sam:2,7,8,10

Task 2

exercise,get up,go jogging,serious,PC games,couch potatoes,suggestions,follow my example,simple and easy

Situation Four

1. The competition has become a global sporting event attended by over half a million people,and watched on television by millions.

2. More than a century.

3. French.

Situation Five

(1)

A:Would you like to go running?

B:I'd enjoy that. Where would you like to go?

A:We could go to the park. There shouldn't be many people now.

B:Good. Let's go.

(2)

A:How about going for a bike ride?

B:Sure. Where?

A:Let's call Harry and ask him. He always knows the best places to go.

B: That's a good idea. I'll get ready.

(3)

A: Let's go swimming.

B: OK. Where should we go?

A: Why don't we go down to the lake? It's not too far from here.

B: Fine. I'll be ready in a minute.

(4)

A: How about going hiking with us?

B: Sounds good to me. Where do you want to go?

A: Let's go up to the mountains. It should be beautiful there.

B: OK. Just give me a few minutes to get ready.

Situation Six

Clerk: Good afternoon, Madam. How can I help you?

Shirley: Well, I am a bit out of shape. I'm thinking about exercising to keep fit.

Clerk: Oh, that's good news for us.

Shirley: So what do you provide?

Clerk: First of all, we'll design a custom-made work-out plan according to your habits.

Shirley: How can I get that done?

Clerk: Well, you have a qualified personal trainer assigned to you. He will give you a fitness assessment and then come up with the work-out plan for your needs.

Shirley: What else?

Clerk: Since everyone is different, your personal trainer will find you suitable exercise equipment and teach you all the techniques to help you achieve your fitness level and goals.

Shirley: Sounds pretty good. How much does it cost?

Clerk: It depends. We offer memberships for one month, half a year and one year.

Shirley: Maybe I'll do one month. Just have a try first—not too tough at the beginning.

Clerk: Wise decision. You'll find it's totally worthwhile.

Shirley: How about time?

Clerk: We are open from 6 A. M. to midnight. You are welcome anytime.

Shirley:Thank you.

Situation Seven

Task 1

1. By what Americans are playing.
2. Five(surfing,sailing,scuba driving,swimming and water skiing).
3. Frozen ponds and ice rinks.
4. Sports widow.
5. Advertisement.

Task 2

1. The shop sells a variety of CDs.
2. He revels in country life.
3. She took delight in betting with me.
4. His face was glued to the window.
5. You must live up to your promise.

Situation Eight

Task 2

POSTER

This Week's Film— *Schindler's List*

Time:6P. M. , May 10
Place:Lecture Hall

The School Students' Union

MEETING NOTICE

November 5th

The last Board of Directors of this year will be held at 10 A. M. on December 1 in the conference room. All directors are requested to be present. The meeting will offer lunch. If anybody is unable to attend,please call before November 15th.

General Manager Office

Keys to Item Five

Warm-up Activities

Open-ended.

Situation One

We all know that health is important, but many people do not pay much attention on their health unless they are ill. I think that this is terribly wrong, because if we are ill, we cannot do anything but take medicine or stay in hospital.

With good health, we can enjoy good food and nice drink. Without good health, no food is delicious, and no drink is tasty.

With good health, we can work well, study well. Without it, we cannot achieve our goal; neither can we acquire knowledge as easily as before.

With good health, we will feel confident and keep an open-mind. Without it, we may feel unconfident or fall into self-pity.

Situation Two

He has a terrible headache. Yesterday he had a running nose. Now his nose is stuffed up, his throat is inflamed and his tongue is thickly coated.

Situation Three

1. They are talking about how to prevent A/H1N1 flu.

2. It's a contagious disease and quite often causes death.

3. Wear gauze mask, open the windows and doors, and wash hands as much as you can, cover your cough, don't touch your face and stay away from people who are sick.

Situation Four

Task 1

eight, minimum, depend on, improved, tide, nutrition, what you need, normal

Task 2

1. Because conflicting advice in recent headlines appears to contradict the old

"8-a-day" advice we all grew up with.

2. You should drink as much water as what you need.

3. The only way is to install a good water filtration system in your home.

Situation Five

Open-ended.

Situation Six

Task 1

1. C   2. B   3. D   4. B

Task 2

1. It is funded by taxation.

2. You should register with a GP as soon as possible so that you can get medical care if you need.

3. If a patient needs to see a specialist doctor, he must first go to his GP and then the GP will make an appointment for the patient to see a specialist at a hospital or clinic.

Task 3

Open-ended.

Situation Seven

Task 2

Dear Sir,

Please excuse my absence from class today, because I've had a headache and a cough. I didn't sleep well in the night. I felt even worse this morning. Therefore, I had to go to the doctor to have myself thoroughly examined. The doctor told me to have a good rest, or it would get serious. So I would like to stay in bed for two days. Thus, I am writing to ask you for two days' sick leave and assure that I will go back to school as soon as possible. Thank you.

Sincerely,

Sophia

Keys to Item Six

Situation One

Open-ended.

Situation Two

fun, positive, Whatever, specific, the real world, practice, access to, download, free

Situation Three

Open-ended.

Situation Four

Open-ended.

Situation Five

Open-ended.

Situation Six

Task 1

1. F   2. T   3. F   4. T   5. T

Task 2

Open-ended.

Task 3

1. With only a few clicks of the mouse, you can go online to buy just about anything you want.

2. Shopping on the Internet can be economical, convenient and safe.

3. The holiday shopping season has already begun.

4. Women make up a larger percentage than men of those who have already started their holiday shopping.

5. I expect to shop and buy more on line this year than last year.

Situation Seven

Task 2

From:	hanmei012@ 163. com
To:	daili-rose@ 126. com
Subject:	Network-based Learning
Date:	April 20th, 2009

Dear Dai Li,

Would you like to hone your professional skills from the comfort of your home or get a college degree without setting feet on campus? There are now thousands of online classes available on the World Wide Web and the number will soon mushroom into tens of thousands.

For decades, students have turned to distance learning to realize their educational goals including correspondence courses. Distance learning has served the needs of people who cannot physically attend classes. With the explosion of information technology and the Internet, you can now have a virtual classroom right on your desktop. In most cases, to take a course you need only your computer, a web browser and Internet access.

Yours sincerely,

Han Mei

Keys to Item Seven

Warm-up Activities

Depending on personal experience, personality types and emotional concern, different people may have different opinions on what education is. Some believe that education is to finish high school or college or regard it as a job-secured means, while others hold that education is a lifelong process. And I support the latter with my reasons as follows.

Education starts with the first breath of the child. Joseph Addison says "What sculpture is to a block of marble, education is to the soul. " A baby absorbs information at the moment he was born. He learns to communicate with his mum, dad and a totally new world as well. Parents' words and behavior are much of importance to him. If early education could be a sort of amusement, one will then be better able to find out the natural bent. The preschool education, crucial to one's personality and intelligence development, forms an indispensable part of the lifelong process, although it is hardly noticeable.

Secondly, one has much more to learn even after he or she has got the highest degree in universities. A college diploma does not mean you are educated. Quite the contrary, it means that you have been opened up to a perpetual state of ignorance and thus a lifelong hunger for more ideas, more knowledge, more good thoughts, more challenges, more of everything. The world is changing at every second and no one can afford to stop learning new things upon graduating from universities, especially teachers. For example, as a teacher of English, profession knowledge is as necessary as up-to-date information of other subjects. The rapid renewal of teaching materials is impelling teachers to renew their knowledge structure and improve themselves otherwise they will be left behind the times.

Education is not only from books or campus but also from daily life. How to survive furious competition in the society is a crucial problem for anyone. People have to learn some necessary skills such as basic computer operation and the techniques of communication with others.

Of course, the primary purpose of education is not only "to teach you how to earn your bread, but to make every mouthful sweeter", according to a famous writer. In a narrow sense, education involves teaching people various subjects or being taught. In fact, the definition of this word is far from that. It is a lifelong process.

Situation One

1. When talking about "Lifelong Education", we must focus on the meaning of life which may last nearly one century for a human being. Only when we keep on looking forward, keep curious about the world after graduation from schools, our lives can be made happy, valuable and even wonderful.

Education helps me open my mind to acquire knowledge, to understand others, to know the changing world. Technique I learned today will definitely be out of date in the future, maybe when I am 30 or 40 years old. I do not want to fall behind. I want to be updated as well as the world.

So,"Lifelong Education" means a lot. It has a great impact on my mental world. It helps me to keep a smart brain. Don't forget education technologies are various. I will take advantage of the Internet to get the latest global news. And, reading suits adult very much because of both of its educational function and its function to help people relax.

2. It's true that education helps people to get good jobs to meet their basic need. But, what's more important, education gives people the method to think, the way to develop both mentally and physically. This makes a difference. Maybe a man without a good education background can be very successful on business or some other fields, but he or she may lose the opportunity to know how beautiful the world is. In my point of view, education's main goal is to improve people which means helping people to think about themselves, think about others, think about the current world and think about the past and the future. Education really makes difference.

Situation Two

Ken wanted to learn business management course.

Situation Three

1. A lecture on English culture.
2. Because there is a lot of work to do. He has already handed in five essays and he has a term paper to write.

Situation Four

1. T 2. T 3. F 4. T 5. F 6. F

Situation Five

Open-ended.

Situation Six

Open-ended.

Situation Seven

Task 1

D

Task 2

1. refers to	2. As it is	3. expand	4. available
5. for the sake of	6. in his case	7. make a point	8. on her doorstep
9. in itself	10. make sure		

Task 3

1. The chances are that they got the wrong password, so we couldn't log into this website.

2. In 1990, she graduated from Guangzhou Foreign Trade University with a bachelor's degree in Economics.

3. I'm not saying that we shouldn't enjoy ourselves, but at some point in our lives we have to work hard.

4. You must keep on learning in order to expand your minds, only by this can you survive in the challenging world.

5. Unless he can immediately change his bad habit of telling lies, he will have to keep hunting jobs all the time.

Situation Eight

Task 1

Sample 1

精彩激烈的女子排球赛

辽宁女排将在我市挑战八一女排！两队都有雄厚的实力和一流的队员。中央电视台体育频道届时将实况转播此场比赛。

时间：1 月 3 日（星期二）下午 1:30

地点：奥林匹克体育馆

Sample 2

端午节龙舟比赛

作为春季运动会的一个项目，也为了欢度中国传统的端午节，我校九个系之间要开展一场龙舟友谊赛。请各位届时光临，为桨手们加油鼓劲并享受春日和煦的阳光。

时间：2010 年 5 月 5 日，下午 3:30

地点：迷人的东湖

Task 2

Exciting INTERNATIONAL FOOTBALL MATCH
China Vs Germany

Place：Capital Gymnasium

Time：3：30 P. M. ，April 28，2010

Please apply at Reception Office for tickets.

Come and cheer for them!

Keys to Item Eight

Situation One

Task 1

Open-ended.

Task 2

1. Good to the last drop. （Maxwell）

2. Time is what you make of it. （Swatch）

3. Connecting people. （Nokia）

4. We lead. Others copy. （Ricoh）

5. The relentless pursuit of perfection. （Lexus）

6. A diamond lasts forever. （De Bierres）

7. World in hand，Soul in Cyber. （Microsoft）

8. Apple thinks different. （Apple）

9. A fair skin now，Dabao knows how. （Dabao）

10. Mosquito Bye Bye Bye. （RADAR）

11. Start ahead. （Rejoice）

12. Newton was wrong. （Triumph）

Situation Two

1. C　2. B　3. D　4. C　5. A

Situation Three

1. Because he advertised the ad，and gained a lot of money.

2. Open-ended.

3. Because they believe celebrity effect can give them more money back.

4. Open-ended.

Situation Four

1. A customer's buying behavior

2. the lifestyle

3. fashion sense, appeal, awareness, fame and public image

4. the right charity work or product.

5. nearly twenty percent

6. the previous identity

7. sustain the interest of the customers

8. conflict with each other

9. his taste for hairstyles

10. a bald look

Situation Five

Task 1

Pros: (1) Advertising is informative.

(2) Ads produce positive image of a product, make the product attractive, and create consumer brand loyalty.

(3) Advertising helps compare things I want to buy, helps companies introduce new products, and helps companies sell more products.

Cons: (1) Advertisements are everywhere. Too much advertising confuses customers.

(2) Pop-up advertising is disturbing.

(3) Ads are misleading sometimes. Ads influence your choices. Ads make a hype about goods.

Task 2

Open-ended.

Situation Six

Task 1

1. We have often been persuaded to buy something because the ad says it's good.

2. We need to pay more for the products because manufacturers spend a load of

money advertising,and the cost of the ads is built into the products.

3. Grace bought the jeans only at 30% off because she didn't keep an eye out for hidden information.

Task 2

Open-ended.

Situation Seven

Task 1

1. C 2. B 3. F 4. E 5. D 6. A

Task 2

Ideas	Details
Advertising is a form of communication.	Communicate a message includes the name of the product or service and how that product or service could potentially benefit the consumer. Persuade potential customers to purchase a product or service.
Media used to deliver advertising messages.	Different types of media. Traditional media such as newspapers, magazines, television, radio, billboards or direct mail.
Organizations that spend money on advertising.	Political parties, interest groups, religious organizations and governmental agencies.
Money spent on advertising in recent years .	Increased. In 2007,more than $150 billion in the United States and $385 billion estimated worldwide. Exceed $450 billion by 2010.

Task 3

1. 广告就是一种交流,它可以影响个人购买某种产品或服务,引导个人支持政治候选人或政治主张。

2. 广告传达产品或服务名称等信息。

3. 广告促使潜在客户去购买或使用某种商品或服务品牌。

4. 在 19 世纪末和 20 世纪初，现代广告随大众产品的逐渐增多而不断发展。

5. 商业广告家通常会寻求自己产品或服务的销售的增长。

Situation Eight

Task 1

Open-ended.

Information for reference:

Writing an ad? The tips below—and the important warning that follows—will help you to get the very best response.

Start by choosing a single benefit of your product or service that you wish to highlight above everything else. This is your "principle selling position" or PSP. To choose this, ask yourself what specific benefit makes your product or service different, better, or special. Is it the price? The convenience? The reliability?

Write attention—grabbing headlines. This is very important. People are overloaded with information, so they skim read, particularly on the Internet. If your headline doesn't get their attention everything else is probably wasted because it won't be read. Your headline will often be based around your PSP.

Write a list of all the features of your product or service then translate each of these into a benefit for the customer. One way to do this is to look at each feature in turn then ask yourself "So what?" Imagine you're a customer, why should you care about this feature? Ask "What will it do for me?"

Write copy that emphasizes the benefits in a way that makes an emotional connection.

Start with your strongest selling points. The first few paragraphs are particularly important. Use them to create a desire for your product or service by briefly touching on the major benefits it will bring the customer. You don't have to go into too much detail up front as you can expand on these benefits later. Do try to get your big guns in early, though.

Testimonials sell. Good, believable testimonials from real people will help sales, particularly on the web where establishing credibility is a tough job. For even better credibility, ask your testimonial writers if you can include their contact details along with their testimonial.

Write with a natural style. Don't try to be pretentious or over friendly. Just write it the way you'd say it.

Decide who you're writing for and why. What tone are you trying to convey:

Lighthearted? Serious? What level of jargon are you going to employ? Suit your language to your intended audience.

The final sales pitch, when it comes, must have three specific parts:

◇ It must incorporate a good deal; e. g. "40% off!"

◇ It must be urgent; e. g. "Only seven more days!"

◇ It must be risk free; e. g. "Backed by a 90-day, no-questions-asked, money-back guarantee!"

End by telling the reader what to do; e. g. "Ring now" or "Click here to order now for immediate delivery!" Needless to say, ordering details must be clearly visible and simple to follow.

Task 2

Open-ended.

Keys to Item Nine

Warm-up Activities

(1) The location.

(2) The quality of service.

(3) Parking or transportation.

(4) AAA ratings.

(5) Rates and discounts.

Situation One

Task 1

They serve good food in this restaurant.

What do you recommend? 您能推荐一些特色菜吗?

What's good there?

Which would you rather have—steak or fish? 你要吃什么——牛排还是鱼?

What would you like to eat?

What kind of vegetables do you have?

barbecue 烤肉

soup 汤

appetizer 开胃品

main course 主菜

dessert 甜点

tea and coffee 茶和咖啡

Task 2

Operator: Hello, Chunky Meat Restaurant, may I help you?

Mr. Smith: I'd like to make a reservation for tomorrow night if possible.

Operator: What time will you arrive?

Mr. Smith: How about a quarter to eight?

Operator: I am terribly sorry, we are all booked up at that time. How about half past nine?

Mr. Smith: Sure, that will be fine.

Operator: How many in your party?

Mr. Smith: There will be four of us.

Operator: Smoking section or non-smoking section?

Mr. Smith: Of course, non-smoking.

Operator: Would you like a table or a booth?

Mr. Smith: A soft booth, near a window, please.

Operator: How will you pay? Cash, check or charge?

Mr. Smith: All I have is cash, is that all right?

Operator: No problem. Do you have any questions for us?

Mr. Smith: What kind of food do you serve?

Operator: We are an upscale European restaurant.

Mr. Smith: Thanks.

Operator: What name shall I put the reservation under?

Mr. Smith: My name is Bubba Smith.

Operator: You are all set, Mr. Smith.

Mr. Smith: Thanks a bunch.

Operator: Anytime.

Situation Two

Task 1

Open-ended.

Task 2

1. March 20th.
2. A non-smoking room.
3. It's too expensive.
4. 88 dollars.
5. Maexner.

Situation Three

Task 1

Open-ended.

Task 2

1. A single room.

2. Yes, she had made a reservation.

3. Fill in the registration form first.

Situation Four

Task 1

1. C   2. A   3. C   4. B

Task 2

1. 632   2. well organized/ a great success

3. Hong Kong   4. credit card   5. sightseeing

Situation Five

Task 1

The hotel needs to check the fact, but the hotel may not have to compensate for this. The customer has left the hotel. Of course, students can hold their own ideas if they have their reasonable views.

Task 2

1. Avoid the use of Never.

2. Avoid the use of Always.

3. Refrain from saying you are wrong.

4. You can say your idea is mistaken.

5. Don't disagree with obvious truths.

6. Attack the idea not the person.

7. Use many rather than most.

8. Avoid exaggeration.

9. Use some rather than many.

10. The use of often allows for exceptions.

11. The use of generally allows for exceptions.

12. Quote sources and numbers.

13. If it is just an opinion, admit it.

14. Do not present opinion as facts.

15. Smile when disagreeing.

16. Stress the positive.

17. You do not need to win every battle to win the war.

18. Concede minor or trivial points.

19. Avoid bickering, quarreling, and wrangling.

20. Watch your tone of voice.

21. Don't win a debate and lose a friend.

22. Keep your perspective—you're just debating.

You need to be very polite when disagreeing with someone in English, even someone you know quite well.

With someone you know very well, you can disagree more directly.

Situation Six

Task 1

Waiter: Hello, may I take your order?

Mary: I'd like the Big Mac Value Meal.

Waiter: What would you like to drink with that?

Mary: Give me a coke.

Waiter: Would you like to upgrade your meal to a supervalue meal?

Mary: No, thanks.

Waiter: Can I get you anything else?

Mary: No, that's it.

Waiter: Is that for here or to go?

Mary: To go.

Waiter: Your total is $4.59.

Task 2

The Fly is a problem, and if you and your representatives do not know how to react positively for the customer immediately, you are not going to turn a fly in the soup into a sale.

You do not have to give your products and services away as this waitress did, but you must do something, immediately to regain the customer's trust. There are just too many other places for your customers to purchase your products and services for you to neglect the need to be prepared to turn a fly in the soup into a loyal customer.

Two ways to prepare for your "Flies" in the soup.

(1)Predetermine what to do.

A. Write down all the obvious negative (flies in the soup) situations that have arisen or may arise. Do this with all of your representative (sales professionals, delivery personnel, cleaning crew, etc.).

B. Let them help you come up with actions to take when these situations arise. Actions can be done on the spot as the flies in the soup situations happen, and actions can be done without anyone else's approval.

(2)100% Customer-centered.

It is very easy to turn a fly in the soup into a lifelong customer if everyone in your organization is 100% Customer-Centered.

When your business is 100% Customer-Centered, everything you say and do will be about the customer, not about you.

Situation Seven

Task 1

1. F　2. F　3. F　4. T

Task 2

1. From hotel to motel.

2. Services and amenities.

3. Budget hotels are designed for travelers looking to minimize their expenses. Business hotels are designed for business travelers. Luxury hotels are designed for those who can afford and purse a high-standard life.

Task 3

1. You only need to fill out a form to get your membership which entitles you to a discount on goods.

2. The minimum charge for hotel limousine is 240 RMB every 2 hours.

3. Our hotel provides an excellent Room Service.

4. We have a special rate for group reservation.

Situation Eight

Task 1

Hotel Registration Form

Check-in Date (入住日期)＿＿＿＿＿＿＿＿

NAME(姓名)＿＿＿＿＿＿＿＿＿＿

PHONE(联系电话)_____   FAX（传真)_____

ADDRESS(地址)_____

CITY(城市)_____   ZIP(邮编)_____

NUMBER OF PEOPLE（入住人数)_____

NUMBER OF BEDS REQUESTED(需要的床位)_____

ROOM TYPE * （see below)(房间类型)_____

SECOND CHOICE(第二选择))_____

ARRIVAL DATE(到达时间) _____

DEPARTURE DATE（离开时间)_____

All reservations must be guaranteed by a credit card or a deposit for the first night's room rate.（预定均须提供信用卡担保或交纳第一晚的定金。)

CREDIT CARD TYPE & NUMBER：(信用卡类型及卡号)

_____

CREDIT CARD SIGNATURE：(信用卡签名)

_____

CREDIT CARD EXPIRATION DATE：(信用卡过期时间)

_____

ENCLOSED：

RESERVATIONS RECEIVED AFTER JANUARY 8，2005，WILL BE PRO-VIDED ON A SPACE AVAILABLE BASIS.

PLEASE NOTE：In the event of cancellation，you must notify the Reservations Department fourteen（14）days prior to arrival. This will avoid a one-night no-show charge.

* ROOM TYPE SELECTIONS：

Oceanfront   @ $ 140 per room

Non-oceanfront   @ $ 125 per room

PLEASE RETURN THIS FORM TO

The King and Prince Beach & Golf Resort

Reservations Department

P. O. Box 20798

St. Simons Island，GA 31522   FAX：912-638-7699

Task 2

HOW WAS YOUR RESERVATION MADE?	
Wonderful Hotel Reservation Office	Wonderful Hotel Website　酒店网站
The Hotel Directly	Other Website　　　　其他网站
Group Reservation　　团体预订	Airline　　　　　是否飞机抵达
Travel Agent　　　　旅行社	Other Methods　　　其他方式
Was the information concerning your reservation correct?　　Yes(　)　No(　)	
Are you traveling on：(旅行原因) Meeting/Conference/Individual Business/Pleasure Combination / Pleasure	
* Your Name：(姓名)	
Reply Address：(回信地址)	
* E-mail：(电子邮箱)	
Phone Number：(电话号码)	
Room No：(房间号码)	Date of Stay：(入住期间)
DURING YOUR VISIT	
Was your room clean and well maintained? 房间干净整洁吗？　Yes(　)　No(　)	
Was the hotel clean and well maintained? 酒店干净整洁吗？　　Yes(　)　No(　)	
Was everything in your room in working order? 房间设备运转正常吗？ 　　　　　　　　　　　　　　　　　　　　Yes(　)　No(　)	
Was the lighting in your room sufficient? 灯光亮吗？　　　　Yes(　)　No(　)	
Did we make you feel safe and secure? 我们使您获得安全感了吗？ 　　　　　　　　　　　　　　　　　　　　Yes(　)　No(　)	
Did we handle your requests efficiently? 我们满足了您的请求吗？ 　　　　　　　　　　　　　　　　　　　　Yes(　)　No(　)	

Would you like to see anything added to your room?   Yes( ) No( )
Whenever our staff interacted with you, did they present themselves in a pleasant and welcome manner?   Yes( ) No( )
Perform their duties promptly and efficiently?   Yes( ) No( )
Prove to be knowledgeable about the hotel and its services? Yes( ) No( )
Fulfill your requests and show commitment to your complete satisfaction?   Yes( ) No( )
Will you want to come back and to recommend the hotel to others? 下次您会继续入住并推荐给朋友吗?   Yes( ) No( )
How satisfied are you with your stay? 您对本次入住的满意度。   Unacceptable or Outstanding
Are there any suggestions or comments you would like to add? 其他建议。

Keys to Item Ten

Warm-up Activities

Saxophone, flute, violin, trombone, piano

Situation One

Open-ended.

Situation Two

Task 1

1. Over 70 countries.

2. Yes, the Philharmonic plays the works of the Johann Strauss family and its contemporaries.

3. The concert wants to send people all over the world a New Year's greeting

in the spirit of hope, friendship and peace.

Task 2

Open-ended.

Situation Three

Task 1

1. T   2. T   3. F   4. T   5. F

Task 2

1. Yes, it is. Because most of all over the world are very proud of winning the trophy.

2. The first Grammy Award telecast took place on the night of November 29, 1959.

3. The Grammy Award is praised for outstanding achievements in the music industry.

Situation Four

Task 1

religious, music, happiness, real-life, sound, governess, household, caring for, fall in love, invade

Task 2

Open-ended.

Situation Five

Nowadays, there is no doubt that Jay Chou becomes more and more popular in R&B music that was born on the 18th Jan., 1979 in Taiwan. And he can play the piano. Luckily, I can play the piano, too. So I hope I can play the piano with him one day.

I love listening to Jay's songs very much. He loves his mother very much. His fourth Music Video was named after his mother's name—Ye Huimei. Thus it can be seen that he is a dutiful son.

Now all of his fans, including me, are crazy about both his handsome and talent!

I like listening to his music alone when I'm sad. Then I usually sit down in my bedroom and turn on the radio. It seems that his songs can express my thoughts and feelings.

Situation Six

Task 1

1. T   2. F   3. T   4. F   5. T

Task 2

1. People use music to express feelings and ideas.

2. Music forms an important part of many cultural and social activities.

3. Music serves to entertain and relax.

4. People probably started to sing as soon as language developed.

5. There are two chief kinds of Western music, classical and popular.

Task 3

Open-ended.

Situation Seven

Task 2

Open-ended.

Keys to Item Eleven

Situation One

Open-ended.

Situation Two

Column A

1. (g, h)

2. (e, f)

3. (d, c)

4. (a, b)

Situation Three

characteristics, behave, abilities, long-term, enable

Situation Four

enthusiastic, weaknesses, cooperative, leisure, energetic

Situation Five

Job Interview Tips

Practice

Practice answering interview questions and practice your responses to the typical job interview questions and answers most employers ask. Think of actual examples you can use to describe your skills. Providing evidence of your successes is a great way to promote your candidacy.

Prepare

Prepare a response so you are ready for the question "What do you know about our company?" Know the interviewer's name and use it during the job interview. If you're not sure of the name, call and ask prior to the interview. Try to relate what you know about the company when answering questions.

Watch

Take a look at my Job Interview Tips Videos, so you'll be sure to amaze a potential employer and leave the right impression.

Get Ready

Make sure your interview attire(服装) is neat, tidy and appropriate for the type of firm you are interviewing with. Bring a nice portfolio with copies of your resume. Include a pen and paper for note taking.

Be on Time

Be on time for the interview. On time means five to ten minutes early. If need be, take some time to drive to the office ahead of time so you know exactly where you are going and how long it will take to get there.

Stay Calm

During the job interview try to relax and stay as calm as possible. Take a moment to regroup. Maintain eye contact with the interviewer. Listen to the entire question before you answer and pay attention—you will be embarrassed if you forget the question!

Show What You Know

Try to relate what you know about the company when answering questions. When discussing your career accomplishments, match them to what the company is looking for.

Follow Up

Always follow up with a thank-you note reiterating(反复地说，重申)your interest in the position. If you interview with multiple people send each one a thank-you note.

Situation Six

As you can see, employers and recruiters are making good use of the Internet and so should you. Some tips will help you learn how to use the net as a job search tool. You may even use it to search for a job already. These tips are to help you make full use of what this amazing tool has to offer.

Be selective for search web site.

There are more job sites than anyone can use productively. Be selective and use niche job boards that focus on your interests and geographic location.

Use search words efficiently.

Searching for a job online is a numbers game. Please Never Forget This! Volume and quality get results. Force yourself to pick Search Words that will return broader results to ensure that you retrieve more jobs than you might normally have.

Avoid the desire to conduct the most precise search. There are two kinds of errors you can make—apply to the wrong job (which usually results in being ignored and put in a database) or not applying to the right job (usually from not having enough time to find all of the appropriate jobs).

You want to see all jobs that are available.

But you want to see them as few times as possible. Refining your Search Words or creating strings will hopefully reduce the number of times you see the same job on a job board.

Create your career networking.

Your career network should include anyone who can assist you with a job search or career move. It can include past and present co-workers, bosses, friends with similar interests, colleagues from business associations, alumni from your university, or acquaintances you have met via online networking services. Your network can also include family, neighbors, and anyone who might have a connection that will help.

Use online resume bank.

1. Prepare your resume so that it is scannable.

2. Send a resume in an email message or as an email attachment.

3. Post an e-resume by filling out an electronic form on company, coop, or job search web sites.

4. Create your own web site and post your resume on it using HTML.

Situation Seven

Task 1

1. career, job
2. despair
3. network
4. reputation
5. stardom

Task 2

1. You'll risk getting started in a career that holds no real appeal for you, and then you'll have to leave it to find something else.

2. The best strategy for moving on is to recognize the reality of the situation, acknowledge your feelings and find a way to cope productively.

3. Developing relationships with people working in your field means that you're top of mind whenever they hear of a new opportunity.

4. Establish your reputation as a Can-Do, enthusiastic employee. Your boss will quickly come to see you as someone he can count on and a huge asset to the team.

5. Look at your first post-college positions as temporary stops on your career path instead of permanent ones. Don't be in such a rush to get promoted either—you have a long career life ahead of you to shoulder the heavy burden of being on top.

Task 3

1. Don't look for a job haphazardly; otherwise you'll have to leave it to find something else because it holds no appeal for you.

2. Developing extensive relationship with people in your field means you'll have more opportunities.

3. It's yourself not your company who is responsible for your career development.

4. Doing a self-assessment will help you determine which occupation could be a good fit for you.

5. Your first post-college position/job is just a temporary stop on your career path.

Situation Eight

Task 1

1. One sales manager.
2. Chinese citizen, aged 35-40.

With college diploma in Marketing,Economics or related field.

Minimum of 5 years' experiences in sales management.

Proficiency in English speaking and writing.

Willing to travel frequently.

Good at using a computer.

Task 2

A Job Wanted Ad

Castle Hotel is an international five-star tourist hotel under the leadership of Mount Emei Tourism Company Ltd. We are looking for an enthusiastic person to assist in the expansion of the hotel.

The successful applicant will have experience in general hotel work and at least one year's experience as an Assistant Manager.

Applicants need a good knowledge of English and possibly two other languages.

Good salary,bonus,good holidays and excellent prospects for promotion with the company.

Apply in confidence with a full resume and a recent photograph to Mr. Gerry Bateman.

Add. :29 People Street,Mount Emei,Sichuan,P. R. China

Tel. :0833-5526888

Keys to Item Twelve

Warm-up Activities

Open-ended.

Situation One

Task 1

1. A corporate structure is the layout of the various departments,divisions,and job positions that interact to conduct the business of the company.

2. First,the corporate layout helps to define all the areas of responsibility within the company. Besides,a corporate structure also helps to establish a line of communication for employees to utilize. By establishing this line of communication,the corporate structure helps to ensure effective interaction and also minimize time wasted by information moving through the company in a disorganized manner. Lastly,the corporate structure helps to establish a working chain or line of authority.

3. (1) Indicate each employee's area of responsibility and to whom each reports.

(2) Coordinate the division of work and make those divisions clear.

(3) Show the types of work done by the business.

(4) Indicate line of promotion.

Task 2

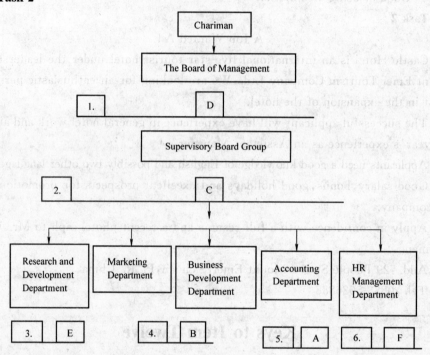

Situation Two

Office Items	Where	What to Do	Work Time
an electric typewriter	on the desk	√ use an electric typewriter	
		√ file letters alphabetically	
all letters	in the filing cabinet	√ keep the confidential file in the safe	9:00 A. M. — 5:30 P. M.
		√ take the clients into the office	
paper and carbon paper	in the cupboard	work with samples	
		do accounting work	
		√ take notes in shorthand	

Situation Three

Task 1

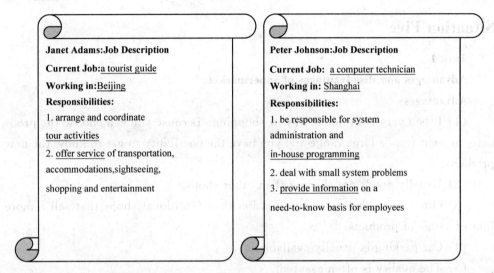

Janet Adams:Job Description

Current Job:a tourist guide

Working in: Beijing

Responsibilities:

1. arrange and coordinate tour activities

2. offer service of transportation, accommodations,sightseeing, shopping and entertainment

Peter Johnson:Job Description

Current Job: a computer technician

Working in: Shanghai

Responsibilities:

1. be responsible for system administration and in-house programming

2. deal with small system problems

3. provide information on a need-to-know basis for employees

Task 2

2. A mechanic：someone whose job is to repair the engines of vehicles and other machines.

3. An electrical engineer：a person who puts in and maintains electrical wires.

4. A firefighter：a person whose job is to stop fires from burning.

5. A flight attendant：someone who serves passengers on an aircraft.

6. A computer programmer：a person whose job is to make produce computer programs.

7. An accountant：someone who keeps or examines the records of money received,paid and owed be a company or a person.

8. A social worker：a person who works for the social services or for a private organization providing help and support for people who need it.

9. An animation designer：a person who makes cartoon pictures or films on computers.

10. A quality inspector：someone whose job is to look at goods when they are being produced to make certain that all the goods are of the intended standard.

Situation Four

Task 1

delightful,a tail, swings from side to side, pulled along gift, $ 34, attractive, wooden,on journeys,softly,hand-painted,$ 32.

Task 2

A&E

Situation Five

Task 1

Advantages and disadvantages of supermarkets

Advantages:

(1) It is a very convenient way of shopping. Because you can choose the product you want from a large range and you have the possibility to get to know the new products.

(2) Usually goods are cheaper than other shops.

(3) Often more choices in one location than traditional shops that sell a more limited range of products.

(4) Car parking is usually available.

(5) The quality is often assured.

(6) They have fresh stock as there would be regular movement of goods.

(7) If you have any complaints you can return your items and replace them.

(8) Shopping becomes a pleasure instead of a chore.

(9) There is also a possibility to pay by cheque or a credit card and vouchers available.

Disadvantages:

(1) If the supermarket is far from your home and you have to carry a lot back, it would be difficult.

(2) Supermarket can be annoying because there is a big choice which can cause confusion.

(3) People often buy unnecessary things because they buy things that they did not plan to buy earlier,seeing to have a good price.

(4) It is time consuming and it takes a while to get there and back.

(5) Big stores are also quite dangerous for all small shops owned by private people,because those shops may be the only source of living of them.

Advantages and disadvantages of small shops

Advantages:

(1) The shop is generally small and has friendly staff.

(2) The staff usually know you very well.

(3) They know what are your favorite products,they can put aside things that

you want to buy but do not have enough money now.

Disadvantages:

(1) The prices are usually uncompetitive.

(2) It is very hard to keep something in secret.

(3) There is little choice.

Task 2

A: Hello, madam, I'm a representative of the Quake Company.

B: Hmm...

A: We're planning on opening a brand new fast-food restaurant in the center of the town. I was just talking to people in the neighborhood and talking to the Neighborhood Committee. Erm... Do you think it would be a good idea... we think that it will create many new jobs.

B: Well, you know, I have talked to my neighbors about this and we really don't want the restaurant.

A: Hmm... but as I say, it will create many new jobs.

B: But our concerns are that the building may be ugly and that also the area around the restaurant may be very noisy.

A: On the contrary, madam, the building is attractive and modern and there will be a playground in the back where children can play.

B: So you're concerned about children?

A: Of course we are.

B: Then why is it that everything your restaurant cooks is not good for people; it's fried and it's greasy...

A: Ah... our research shows that the ones we make are nutritious and good for health.

B: And what about the rubbish? I mean, you're talking about health. What about the rats it will attract and the bad smell in the neighborhood?

A: Hmmm... but madam, think about it. It will make good fast food available to everybody in the neighborhood.

B: But we really have enough places to eat.

Situation Six

Task 2

1. a projector   2. a fax machine   3. a digital camera   4. a shredder

5. a scanner   6. a laser printer   7. a photocopier   8. a laptop

Instruction 1

Steps：

(1) Make sure the machine has been plugged into a power source and also plugged into a working phone jack.

(2) Turn the machine on.

(3) Gather the documents and put them in order.

(4) Fill out a separate piece of paper called a coversheet with the following information：

      recipient's name；

      recipient's fax number/phone number；

      your name；

      your phone number.

(5) Dial the number of the destination machine.

(6) Lay the documents face-up in the machine feeder tray with the coversheet on top.

(7) Dial the recipient's number (dialing instructions for international calls).

(8) Press the "send" button, and the job is done.

Instruction 2

Steps：

(1) Before shooting, check the battery level.

(2) If the battery is exhausted, recharge it for 90 minutes and then insert it into the battery chamber on the bottom of the machine.

(3) Power on the machine.

(4) Look through the viewfinder and adjust focus by sliding the diopter control up and down.

(5) Frame the picture with the subject in at least one of the three focus areas in the viewfinder .

(6) Press the shutter-release button and shoot.

Warnings

Protect the lens from water, sweat and dust.

Instruction 3

Steps：

(1) Bring white screen down.

(2) Using remote control, turn on the equipment by pressing the "Operate" button for several seconds until you see a small green light blinking on the equipment.

(3) Press "Computer".

(4) Connect one end of the VGA cable to the laptop and connect the other end to "VGA" jack.

(5) Turn on the laptop.

(6) Wait until you see the computer screen on both monitor and white screen.

(7) Using remote: press the "Operate" button for several seconds to turn off the equipment.

(8) Roll up the white screen by pressing "UP" on black button on the wall.

(9) Turn off your computer.

Possible Problems:

(1) There appears a blue screen with the words "No Signal".

(2) No Sound from laptop to the equipment.

Solution 1:

Check whether you have pressed the "Computer" or "RGB" button on the equipment's remote control long or hard enough.

Solution 2:

Check that all cables are fully plugged in. Check sound volume on laptop and the equipment.

Situation Seven

Task 1

1. T   2. F   3. F   4. T   5. F   6. T

Task 2

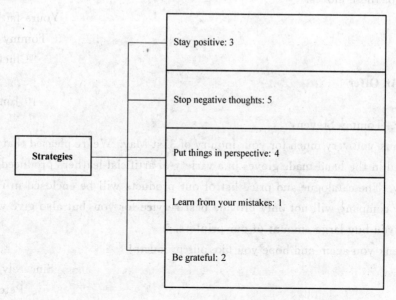

Task 3: Translation

1. Changing your attitude towards work won't necessarily happen overnight.

2. You'll be fined if you are caught smoking in the office.

3. "Reframing" can help you find the good in a bad situation.

4. Gratitude can help you focus on what's positive about your job.

5. Being positive will help you manage your stress and experience the rewards of your profession.

Situation Eight

Task 2

1. An inquiry

31 May,2009

Kim & Co. ,Ltd.

46 Raden Street

London, UK

Dear Sirs,

We learn from Thomas H. Pennie of New York that you are producing hand-made gloves in a variety of artificial leathers. There is a steady demand here for gloves of high quality at moderate prices.

Will you please send me a copy of your glove catalogue, with details of your prices and terms of payment? I should find it most helpful if you could also supply samples of these gloves.

Yours faithfully,

Tommy Steven

Chief Buyer

2. An Offer

10 June,2009

Dear Mr. Tommy Steven,

Thank you very much for your inquiry of 31st May. We're pleased that you're interested in the hand-made gloves in a variety of artificial leathers produced by our company. The catalogue and price list of our products will be enclosed in this letter. Our company will not only provide best service for you, but also give you discount if you buy large amount of our printers.

Thank you again and hope you like our products!

Sincerely yours,

Peter Kevil

Keys to Item Thirteen

Warm-up Activities

Open-ended.

Situation One

1. The man talked about some tips about how to prepare starting business.

2. What is a perfect idea? Each individual entrepreneur has his concept of the perfect business. Each perfect business is defined by the business owners. Keeping this in mind, let's start on my five concepts of finding the perfect business.

Number One—Understanding your customer. This might seem strange to start here as how you know your customers before you have a business idea in place. The answer is simple—your customers make the business, therefore without customers there is no business.

Number Two—Passion. Passion here does not mean being fanatical(狂热的) about your product or service. But, it does mean having some interest in what you do.

Number Three—Understand Your Competition. Every business has competition directly or indirectly.

Number Four—Cash Flow. Lots of entrepreneurs enter the business world with great ideas but very poor understanding of the capital it will take to get their venture off the ground. Knowing your total cash flow will help ensure that all of your costs (variable and fixed) can be covered by the business—the perfect business idea.

Number Five—You. Know who you are. Know your strengths and weaknesses. Know that you are ready, willing and able to do what it takes to make your venture a success.

3. I want to have my own business. I think I have following good qualities and competences for becoming a boss.

I can afford to quit my job and live on next to nothing for at least 3 years. I have good credit so I can easily get funding for my business for inventory, salaries, etc. I am good at managing my time. I like to train and manage others and I am good at managing people. I always take responsibility for my own success or failure. I have good negotiating skills. I am willing to take risks to achieve my goals. I am willing to work very long hours, including weekends and to forego vacations to get my business up and running. I communicate and work well with others. I have the personnel, partners or resources to fill in the blanks where I don't have the skills to do the job myself and I will be able to afford to pay these people. I am a good sales person. I have enough assets or money to invest a reasonable amount in my own business. I am good at problem solving. I am not afraid to learn new things. I accept setbacks and keep on trying. I know how to set goals and measure results. I can communicate my passion for my business to bankers, lawyers and customers alike.

Situation Two

Column A (Name)	Column B(Suggestion)
Susan	b, c
Helen	a, d
The art people	e

Situation Three

goal, options, chance, personal, storm

Situation Four

1. She is busy with studying personal development.

2. Her career goal is to be a successful business woman, and have her own company.

3. She should have self-confidence, have goals, positive attitude, good communication, and so on. She will match her personality with her career goals, and make a plan. She needs more knowledge, and she needs to realize her interest, ability, characteristic to unite the practice. She must raise herself to adapt to the environment around her. Try her best to do everything well.

Situation Five

A person must have such qualities as becoming honest, hard-working, persistent. He has special knowledge of a certain field. He should be in good health and receive higher education. In order to be successful in your own career, you should choose the right business which inspires yourself, makes you happy and meets your customers' needs.

Situation Six

Sample 1:

Maybe you have an idea for an internet business startup, or you are starting a small business from home, need a business startup loan, business startup software, or just want to know the basics of how to write a business plan. Whether you are still in the idea stage of how to start a business, or you've already taken serious steps to starting a business, finding the right advice, resources and entrepreneurial communities will be vital to the success of your small business startup.

Here are four factors that improve the odds of success for anyone who wants to start a small business:

(1) People. If you can afford to hire employees or can bring in partners when you first start a business, DO IT. Studies show that well-staffed business startups have better survival rates than solo operations. If this won't work for you, at least seek out experienced mentors(顾问).

(2) Start-up capital of at least $50,000. Not easy, perhaps, but studies show that businesses starting with less than $50,000 have higher failure rates. That's just the way it is. The key is to have enough financing so your business can take root.

(3) Training. If you can, attend seminars on how to start a small business offered through a local Small Business Development Center, or enroll in a college-based entrepreneurship program to learn the ropes(摸到窍门). You might be the smartest geek in the world, but if you have no business sense, you're in trouble.

(4) Home beginnings. To keep costs low, start a home-based business. Businesses that begin this way and then move into bigger digs(住处)later have higher success rates on starting small business.

Sample 2:

(1) Study yourself. This is the key to career planning. Understanding what you like, what you value, and what you want to become are the foundations for all career planning. In studying yourself, you examine your strengths and your weaknesses, your goals and the trends in your personal development. The self-understanding that you gain enables you to imagine how certain occupations may best fit your personality, interests, abilities, and goals. All career decisions require us to learn both about ourselves and about work, and to integrate these two kinds of knowledge.

(2) Write your career goals down. A technique useful for organizing ideas

about your career development is actually to write them down by time blocks in your life. Writing something down forces you to crystallize(明确) your thinking and to recognize unclear and half-formed ideas. It may lead to new insights into your possibilities and may help you to see new relationships, patterns and trends, or to identify gaps in your thinking about your career development.

(3)Review your plans and progress periodically with another person. Every so often, take stock of your situation and consider what steps have to be taken next. Taking inventory of progress and planning further steps can help you cope with the changes that you undergo and the changes that take place in the labor market. Talking over your plans with a college counselor, your parents, and your friends helps you define your goals and improve your career plans or make them work.

(4)If you choose a career that does not fit you, you can start over. Today, growing numbers of men and women are changing careers or getting second starts in careers that have greater appeal to them. Many of those who find that their line of work is unsatisfactory restrain themselves for a different occupation. Often their new occupation is one that they overlooked when they were young or that they did not have an opportunity to pursue at that time for financial or other reasons.

Sociologists say that there are few changes in careers that involve "downward" movement; most involve the traditional business of "getting ahead". Society no longer attaches the stigma of "instability" to the idea of career hopping, as it once did.

Job changes and career shifts occur at all ages. It has been estimated that as many as one out of four make workers between the ages of 20 to 25 change their lines of work.

Career planning does not guarantee that all the problems, difficulties, or decision-making situations that face you in the future will be solved or made any easier. No formula can be given to do that. But career planning should help you to approach and cope better with new problems, such as deciding whether or not to enter educational or training programs, deciding whether or not to change jobs, and analyzing the difficulties you are having with a situation or a person.

Nobody can foresee what the future holds for any of us. There are social, emotional, and moral considerations in our future that cannot be foreseen. But the most important lesson of this often unhappy modern world is that progress comes from planning. Ignorance about one's career is not bliss; reason is better than chance and fate. Although there is no sure way to make career plans work out, there are things that you can do now to shape your career possibilities.

Situation Seven

Task 1

1. F   2. T   3. T   4. F   5. F   6. T

Task 2

1. The right business is a business that simultaneously inspires you, makes you happy, meets your customers' needs.

2. Consider all your ideas—and those of friends and family—carefully; Many entrepreneurs consider themselves jacks of all trades; The right business for you will be in an industry and a market where there is room for you; Whatever business you choose, you will have to make a living doing it.

Task 3

1. You must be passionate about your ideas in order to make them fly.

2. If you can't fit the requirements of society, you must get out of the game.

3. Career planning includes gathering information about ourselves and about occupations, estimating probable outcomes of various courses of action, and finally, choosing alternatives that we find attractive and feasible.

4. Every successful business starts with a great idea, but not all great ideas result in a successful business.

5. The right business for you will be in an industry and a market where there is room for you.

Situation Eight

Task 2

	Schedule
Saturday Nov. 18	7:30 Meet in the hotel lobby(在宾馆大厅集合) 7:45 Take coach to Zhongshan Museum 11:10—11:40 Tour around the city by coach(乘车游览市区) 12:00 Have lunch in the hotel(在宾馆吃午餐) 14:00 Take coach to Lingyin Temple 17:30 Dinner party(晚宴)
Sunday Nov. 19	8:30 Take coach to Confusian Temple 11:30 Have lunch at one restaurant 14:00 Go shopping downtown(前往市中心购物) 17:00 Dinner at Nanjing Restaurant 19:00 To the Railway Station(去火车站)

Keys to Item Fourteen

Warm-up Activities

Yin/Macau Dollar/Euro Dollar/US Dollar/Hong Kong Dollar/
Pound/Franc/Australia Dollar/RMB

Situation One

There are such accesses to investment like buying stocks, investing in housing, investing in insurance, saving money in banks and so on.

Situation Two

First fill out a deposit slip, and then input the secret code. At last get the check slip and the passbook.

Situation Three

She wants to buy 1,000 shares of Lenovo.

Situation Four

They will pay if certain types of losses occur to the policyholder according to the policy.

Situation Five

Open-ended.

Situation Six

Task 1
1. T　2. F　3. F　4. T　5. T
Task 2
Open-ended.
Task 3
1. Which would you prefer, fixed deposit or current deposit?

2. It is unreasonable to invest regardless of risks.

3. A well thought-out plan can ensure the benefit from your investment.

4. Investors who are more concerned about safety rather than growth often put their money in the bank.

5. Investors who have varied investments may take on less risks.

Situation Seven

Task 2

> Memo
>
> To: the manager of the Sales Department
> From: John Brown
> Date: Sept. 20,2008
> Subject: Computer
>
>   Our office is in a great want of a new computer to keep in touch with the foreign companies, which is approved at the managers' meeting on September 8th. I hope that you will settle it as soon as possible.

Keys to Item Fifteen

Situation One

Arguments

3. Romantic love will enable the couple to conquer any difficulties in their life together.

4. In feudal society, many people suffered from arranged marriages because love was never an element for consideration in marriages at that time.

5. Romantic love can lead to the healthy psychological development of the couple.

6. Marriages based on romantic love will bring forth beautiful and intelligent children.

7. Marriages based on love tend to create a happy and harmonious atmosphere in the family which is good for the development of children.

8. A happy marriage helps one to achieve more in one's career.

9. A marriage without love is worse than being single.

10. Marriages without love are most likely to end in divorce, which creates many social problems.

Counter-arguments

3. Lack of money in a new marriage might bring trouble and chronic quarrelling.

4. A marriage based on romantic love alone will not last long, for a sense of responsibility is most essential to a successful marriage.

5. Age is a very important condition for a happy marriage because, if the couple belong to different age groups, they tend to have different interests and find it hard to understand each other.

6. Love is not the most important condition for a happy marriage, because when the choice is carefully and wisely made, it's usually a good one.

7. Health is a very important condition for a good marriage. If either party of a marriage suffers from poor health, then happiness is impaired.

8. As the saying goes, "Love blinds a man to all imperfections". So a marriage based on love alone is only a bet for happiness.

9. Parental approval is important for marriages because it creates unity in a family. Moreover, the experience of parents can often correct and restrain the headstrong and distorted choices of inexperienced youth.

10. Love is not the single, most important condition for a successful marriage. It requires the combination of many conditions, all of which are important.

Situation Two

Open-ended.

Situation Three

Open-ended.

Situation Four

Open-ended.

Situation Five

Open-ended.

Situation Six

Task 1
1. T 2. T 3. F 4. T 5. F
Task 2
Open-ended.
Task 3
1. Marriage is the result and extension of love.

2. Our children had to have good surroundings to grow up in.

3. Successful marriage is the most effective form of social support.

4. When Catherine was pregnant, she looked like a ball.

5. After the birth of our first child, we always quarreled because of the child and our housework.

Situation Seven

Task 2

1.

Dear Dan and Laura,

Jim and I want to thank you for the beautiful vases. We are looking forward to getting lots of use out of your thoughtful and practical wedding gift.

We are having fun getting organized in our little apartment. Soon we will be ready for company, and we will give you a call. After all the times you have had us over for dinner, we will get to play host for a change.

Thanks again for the lovely gift.

Fondly,
Jim & Mary

2.

Dear Peter,

I am excessively sorry to say that I am just now using the dictionary you mentioned in my teaching work. So I can not lend you this copy. And I tried to buy you another copy of the dictionary from the bookshop but failed to get it. Therefore it is not in my power to comply with your request.

Hoping you may be successful in some other quarter and with a feeling of deep regret at my inability to render you a service.

Yours ever,
Russell

Tapescripts

Item One

Situation Two

Listen to the dialogue twice and finish the task according to requirements.

W: It's a successful conference, isn't it?

M: Yes, really.

W: Let me introduce myself. I'm Mary Wilson.

M: Nice to meet you, Miss Wilson. My name's Tom Johnson.

W: Sorry. What's your surname again, please?

M: Johnson.

W: Well, it's very nice to meet you. Which company do you work for, Mr. Johnson?

M: I'm working for Haier Company.

W: I see. I'm at IBM, in the International section. What department are you in, Mr. Johnson?

M: I'm in charge of the sales and marketing department.

W: Oh, you are a manager. Well, here's the lift. After you.

Situation Three

Listen to the following short passage twice and finish the task according to requirements.

Good evening, everyone. Welcome to our city. You will stay at the Garden Hotel tonight. I hope you'll have a good rest.

Tomorrow, breakfast is served at 7:00 A. M. We'll start off at 7:45 A. M. to visit the Shanghai Radio and TV Tower. And then we'll go to visit the Shanghai Science and Technology Museum and have lunch there. In the afternoon, at about four, we'll go to the Jinmao Building. It is the tallest building in Shanghai. In the evening we'll enjoy the beautiful sights along the Huangpu River by ship.

Situation Four

Listen to the following short passage twice and finish the task according to requirements.

Miss Fang from China worked as a secretary in an American company. She became friends with one of the foreign secretaries, a woman named Caddy Lane from Canada. The two usually had lunch together and Fang often asked Caddy for advice on problems she faced about American society. Caddy gave her a lot of advice and helped her move from one apartment to another. Fang visited Caddy several times at home but she didn't invite Caddy to her apartment, because she shared it with two other persons. If they didn't see each other over the weekends, they usually talked on the telephone.

However, recently something seemed to be going wrong. Caddy seemed to be getting impatient. She started going out by herself at lunch time instead of having with Fang, and she seemed unwilling to answer questions. Fang was puzzled. She couldn't imagine what the problem was.

Item Two

Situation Two

Listen to the dialogue twice and finish the task according to requirements.

Jane: Just look! The day has dawned lovely!

Hank: It certainly looks clear—good day for a picnic.

Jane: I think so.

Hank: Well, how about it then?

Jane: Let's do it. How soon do you want to leave?

Hank: Say...^in an hour.

Jane: Make it an hour and a half. We have to take time to get some food, and besides that I'd like to invite Nancy and Jim.

Hank: Fine. You get things ready in the house. I'll go and pack the car.

Situation Three

Listen to the dialogue twice and finish the task according to requirements.

Anita: Would you like some cookies? I just made them.

Peter: Yes, please. Thank you.

Anita: These are chocolate, and those are almond-flavored.

Peter: I guess I'll try a chocolate first. Mm ... this is delicious. Are they hard to make?

Anita: No, they're really quite easy. Wait a minute, I've got the recipe right here.

See... these are the ingredients, and then you just follow the directions.

Peter: That does look easy. I think I'll make some tonight.

Situation Four

Listen to the following short passage twice and finish the tasks according to requirements.

Western fast food business has developed tremendously in the past 50 years. Nowadays people can see all kinds of fast food restaurants here and there, which clearly shows how close it is related to our daily life. Most people believe that fast food business has become part of our lives and its development is good for both society and people. Firstly, the best thing about fast food is being fast. Now everyone lives a busy life so time is the most valuable thing to us all. Fast food offers a most efficient way to eat. You will waste no time in waiting or choosing. Secondly, fast food restaurants provide us with a good environment for entertainment and study. Friends come here, chatting or playing cards; students come here, reading books or doing homework, and meanwhile you can enjoy a bag of chips and a bottle of cola which will bring more pleasure. Thirdly, youngsters can even find good opportunities of working practice in some fast food restaurants. The working experience helps them understand the society better and improves their communicating skills. In many ways, we benefit a lot from the fast food business.

Item Three

Situation Two

Listen to the dialogue twice and finish the task according to requirements.

Hanks: Good morning, I'd like to book a flight from Beijing to Shanghai, please.

Travel Agent: I see. When are you traveling?

Hanks: I'd like to fly next Friday.

Travel Agent: Is that a return journey or just one-way?

Hanks: One-way, please. I'm flying back to London from Shanghai.

Travel Agent: OK. That will be 1,400 RMB, please.

Hanks: How long is the flight?

Travel Agent: It's about three hours.

Hanks: When is the departure time?

Travel Agent: 9:30 in the morning, but you have to be there one hour in advance.

Hanks: Thanks.

Situation Three

Listen to the dialogue twice and finish the task according to requirements.

Susan: Hi, Mark! Haven't seen you for years!

Mark: Really? Oh, I have just been back from Wuhan.

Susan: Wow, Wuhan? For business?

Mark:Oh,no. Now it's summer vacation, I just went there for a trip.

Susan: How was it?

Mark:Fantastic! I didn't want to come back.

Susan: But I heard that the weather of Wuhan at this time is horrible.

Mark:That's true. It was so hot in summer that people call it one of the four
     stoves in China.

Susan: I hate hot weather! Where did you visit there?

Mark:There're many interesting places to go, such as Mulan Mountain, the East
     lake, but I only had time to visit the Yellow Crane Tower, one of the most
     famous scenic spots in Wuhan.

Susan: The Yellow Crane Tower? I have never heard about it.

Mark:It is said the tower has a history of more than thousands of years. And you
     can overlook the whole city, especially the Yangtze River clearly.

Susan: I heard the food there is wonderful.

Mark:They are. And not only the people are friendly, but also the food is deli-
     cious, not to mention cheap.

Susan: I envy you much.

Mark:Come on, wouldn't it be great if we could go to Wuhan together sometime?

Susan: Yeah, it really would.

Situation Four

Listen to the dialogue twice and finish the task according to requirements.

Guide: It's about half an hour to climb to the top of the mountain.

Man: It is safe, right?

Guide: Yes, you don't have anything to worry about. We do about 10 trips a month up the mountain, and these tours have been going on for over ten years without any accidents. Keep your eyes open for wild animals as we are climbing. It isn't uncommon to see deer and even bears.

Woman: What's that mountain to the left called?

Guide: That's Mount Lotus. And to the right of that with the three small points is Mount Eagle. Now, if you look up straight ahead, you should be able to see a large eagle's nest. Does everyone see it there?

Man: Are there any baby birds?

Guide: That's a good question. I haven't seen any yet, but we usually see them around this time of year.

Woman: What's that lake down there, to the right of the green meadow?

Guide: I'm glad you asked. That's Mirror Lake. It's actually a man-made pond that was built as part of a conservation effort over twenty years ago. During the 1970s, many kinds of wild animals were extinguishing. Since Mirror Lake was built, ducks, swans, and geese have returned to the area.

Man: Is this the highest mountain in this region?

Guide: No, actually, Mount Tianzhu, which we will be able to see in just a minute or so has the highest peak.

Woman: Can you ski throughout the year?

Guide: No, we can only ski in winter. Oh, look everyone. There are two deer feeding on the grass right below us.

Man: Thanks, that should be a great photo.

Item Four

Situation Two

Listen to the dialogue twice and finish the task according to requirements.

Like Parents, Like Children

John: What would you like to do other than work, Jerry?

Jerry: Well, sports might be my hobby.

John: What kind of sports do you like most?

Jerry: I used to like ice-skating, but now I'm interested in table tennis.

John: Actually I like it, too.

Jerry: Really? Whom do you usually play with, John?

John: Usually with my elder brother and younger sister.

Jerry: Where do you go to play? Gymnasium?

John: No, we have a table at home.

Jerry: Lucky you!

John: How come you like table tennis?

Jerry: My parents love it and they always say it's a great sport. Then gradually I found it was really interesting, So now, I like it.

John: Well, it seems that family influence is very important.

Jerry: There you have it.

Situation Three

Listen to the dialogue twice and finish the task according to requirements.

Where There Is a Will, There Is a Way

Sam: You're really fit, Jeff. Do you exercise a lot?

Jeff: Yes, Sam. I always get up very early, and go jogging for an hour.

Sam: You're kidding!

Jeff: No, I'm serious.

Sam: What else do you do after that?

Jeff: After that, I usually lift weights and do bodybuilding for about half an hour.

Sam: Wow! How often do you exercise like that?

Jeff: About four times a week. What about you?

Sam: Well, I seldom do exercise. I usually watch TV and play PC games in my free time.

Jeff: It's not surprising that we have so many couch potatoes.

Same: I really want to start to be fit. Do you have any suggestions for me?

Jeff: Sure, if you can follow my example.

Sam: I guess it's really hard for a beginner.

Jeff: Well, it's not that difficult, in fact.

Sam: What should I do then?

Jeff: You may start with some simple and easy exercise, liking jogging or bicycling.

Sam: Good idea! Thank you.

Situation Four

Listen to the following short passage twice and finish the tasks according to requirements.

Wimbledon is the most important sporting event of the British summer. Since the first tournament was played in 1877 in front of a few hundred spectators, the competition has become a global sporting event attended by over half a million people, and watched on television by millions.

The world's top tennis players agree that playing at Wimbledon is an experience like no other. John McEnroe, a three-time Wimbledon winner, describes Wimbledon as "the hallowed ground of the sport".

Although the Wimbledon tennis championship has been in existence for more than a century, the sport of tennis has a much longer history. Most experts agree that the modern game has its origins in a courtyard ball game played by French monks in the 11th century.

For this reason many of the words used in tennis are of French origin. The unusual terms used in scoring a tennis match are English versions of French words: deuce (pronounced "juice") comes from the French word "deux", meaning " two". The word love , meaning "zero", also has French origins.

Item Five

Situation Two

Listen to the dialogue twice and finish the task according to requirements.

Doctor: Good morning. What's troubling you?

George: Good morning, doctor. My head seems to blow up.

Doctor: All right, young man. Tell me how it got started.

George: Yesterday I had a running nose. Now my nose is stuffed up. I have a sore throat. And I'm afraid I've got a temperature. I feel terrible.

Doctor:Don't worry, young man. Let me give you an examination. First let me take a look at your throat. Open your mouth and say "Ah".

George: Ah.

Doctor:Good. Now put your tongue out. All right, let me examine your chest. Please unbutton your shirt. Let me check your heart and lungs. Take a

deep breath and hold it. Breathe in, and out. By the way, do you have a
history of tuberculosis?

George: No, definitely not.

Doctor: Look, your throat is inflamed. And your tongue is thickly coated. You
have all the symptoms of influenza.

George: What should I do then?

Doctor: A good rest is all you need, and drink more water. Let me give you some
medicine.

George: Thank you very much.

Doctor: That's all right. Remember to take a good rest.

George: I will. Goodbye, doctor.

Doctor: Bye!

Situation Three

Listen to the dialogue twice and finish the task according to requirements.

M: Hi, Lily, what are you busy with nowadays?

W: I'm busy helping people prevent A/H1N1 flu.

M: That's a horrible contagious disease and quite often causes death.

W: Yes, and it became known to all overnight.

M: By the way, what can be done to help prevent it?

W: The first important thing is to wear gauze masks in public places.

M: Why is that?

W: Because masks help keep the virus from going into your nose.

M: What's the second important thing to do?

W: Open the windows and doors as much as possible.

M: So the virus can't stick together in the flowing wind.

W: You get the point.

M: What else can be done to deal with A/H1N1 flu?

W: Wash your hands as much as you can with running water for at least 30 seconds. Cover your cough, don't touch your face and stay away from people who
are sick.

M: In this way, bacteria can't stay on your hands and avoid infecting each other, I
guess.

W: It's a very effective way to protect oneself from A/H1N1 flu.

M: A/H1N1 flu is horrible but not as horrible as people have imagined.

W: It is reported that scientists will be able to invent vaccine to conquer it in the near future.

Situation Four

Listen to the following short passage twice and finish the tasks according to requirements.

Have you ever heard that water is the best medicine for our illnesses? How much water do you really need? Conflicting advice in recent headlines appears to contradict the old "8-a-day" advice we all grew up with. Is it necessary to drink eight glasses of water daily, or is this recommendation exaggerated and out of date?

We've heard for years that eight glasses of water daily is the minimum necessary to keep healthy. Your weight loss and health depend on it. Drink the minimum and you will get clearer skin, better sleep, and improved vision. But, the tide has turned, away from liquid nutrition toward examining your daily diet, including what you eat, as well as what you drink. The answer is that you need what you need! If it's summer, you need more. If you're exercising, you need more. If you're a "normal" person, sitting there, who's not sweating, experts say that you need no more than four glasses of water daily.

It would make sense that the quality of water should be just as important as the quantity. Drinking water should always be clean and free from pollutants to ensure proper health and wellness. According to recent news and reports, we have reached the point that all sources of our drinking water, including municipal water systems, wells, lakes, rivers, and even ice stream, contain some level of pollutants. A good water filtration system installed in your home is the only way to ensure the quality and safety of your drinking water.

Item Six

Situation Two

Listen to the dialogue twice and finish the task according to requirements.

Li Hua: Hi! Zhang Tao, how are you doing?

Zhang Tao: Fine, thanks.

Li Hua: Yeah. What do you usually do on weekends? I feel so bored on weekends.

Zhang Tao: Why don't you surf the Internet? There are so many fun things there.

Li Hua: Well, my mother doesn't let me get on line. She says there are so many
traps on the Internet. She is afraid that I might get bad influence from
those unhealthy sites.

Zhang Tao: She only looks at the negative side of the Internet. Actually there are
far more positive impacts.

Li Hua: Give me some examples, please.

Zhang Tao: Simply by clicking some buttons, you can get information about all
kinds of topics. Whatever you are looking for, you will find it. Even if
you want to have very specific information, you will find it in a short
time.

Li Hua: Tell me some more, please.

Zhang Tao: You can socialize with people. I find that I could find more friends on
the Internet than in the real world.

Li Hua: Really? Sounds interesting.

Zhang Tao: There are social communities on the Internet, too, like English Corners. I often go there to practice my oral English. Another big advantage of the Internet is the easy access to information and it is very
cheap. You may download songs, read novels, play games and so on.
There are many web sites that offer free stuff.

Li Hua: Can I voice chat with you tonight? I want you to tell me more about Internet.

Zhang Tao: Sure. I use QQ. You may download one.

Li Hua: OK. See you on QQ then.

Zhang Tao: See you.

Situation Three

**Listen to the following short passage twice and finish the tasks according to re-
quirements.**

Do you like chatting online? What do you usually chat about with your friends
online? I chat with my friends on different subjects depending on who they are.
With my good friends we usually share our mutual experiences. Sometimes we express our negative and positive feelings. We also help one another by resolving
homework problems. I enjoy chatting on line a lot. It helps me to keep the good
friendship going.

Online chat can be refered to any kind of communication over the Internet, but is primarily meant to refer to direct one-on-one chat or text-based group chat. The expression online-chat comes from the word chat which means "informal conversation". Tencent QQ, generally referred to as QQ, is the most popular free instant messaging computer program in Mainland China.

Situation Four

Listen to the following short passage twice and finish the task according to requirements.

Common Symptoms of Internet Addiction Disorder

With the Internet becoming an ever-present factor in the lives of students all over the world, psychologists have found a new unhealthy mental phenomenon and termed it "Internet Addiction Disorder".

(1) Always be with the Internet in a hurry;

(2) Need to use the Internet with increasing amount of time to achieve satisfaction;

(3) Have no ability to control Internet use;

(4) Restlessness when attempting to cut down on Internet use;

(5) Using Internet as a means to escape from problems;

(6) Tell lies to family/friends about things related to surfing the Internet;

(7) Be harmful to significant relationships, job, educational or career opportunities because of the Internet;

(8) Keep returning even after spending an excessive amount of money on online fees;

(9) Anxiety or increased depression appears when off-line;

(10) Staying on-line longer than originally intended.

Item Seven

Situation Two

Listen to the dialogue twice and finish the task according to requirements.

Diane: What did you do yesterday evening?

Ken: It was Tuesday, remember? I went to my evening class.

Diane: Oh, your business management course. How do you like it?

Ken: I like it very much.

Diane: Are you sure you will pass the course?

Ken: Yes, I'm certain I can get the certificate.

Diane: Do you think the certificate will help you find a better job?

Ken: I don't know. Maybe it will be of some help.

Diane: What do you think of your present job?

Ken: It isn't the worst job in the world, but it isn't the best one, either.

Diane: Do you want to work for a big company?

Ken: I want to get ahead. I want to make more money.

Situation Three

Listen to the dialogue twice and finish the task according to requirements.

Mike: Hi, Diana.

Diana: Hi, Mike! Nice to see you again.

Mike: Me, too. Diana, we have a lecture this afternoon. It's about English cul-
      ture. Would you like to join us?

Diana: Oh, I'd love to, but you know, I have a computer class this afternoon.

Mike: A computer class?

Diana: Yes, it's a compulsory course. Dr. Rich is very strict, and he won't let us
       pass if we are absent from his class three times or more.

Mike: Oh, poor Diana. Do you have business communication class?

Diana: No, not for this term.

Mike: Is it optional or compulsory?

Diana: Optional, I think. And I'll take it next term. By the way, is it difficult?

Mike: Very difficult, I would say. We have a lot of work to do this term and I've
      already handled in five essays.

Diana: Really? Do you have a term paper?

Mike: Yes. A paper with 3,000 words.

Diana: That's torture. Oh, I'm not cut for it.

Mike: Come on! I know you are!

Situation Four

**Listen to the following short passage twice and finish the tasks according to re-
quirements.**

Good morning, everyone. Today we'll discuss some new changes in education.
As we know, we're now in the information age. So what will our school look like
in the future? And what will our students do for their education?

First of all, our classrooms will look very different. We'll certainly see rooms full of computers. Students do most of their class work here. But they will also spend a lot of time at home, on-line, or on the Internet.

Suppose you are a college student in 2010. In the morning, you go to a history lecture in Oxford University which starts at 10 and ends at 12. In the afternoon you go to a lecture on international law from 2 to 5 in the Law School of Yale University. And in the evening you do an experiment from 6 to 9 in a lab of Southeast University. There you can talk to your tutor and your classmates about how to fight the latest computer virus.

Item Eight

Situation Two

Listen to the dialogue twice and finish the task according to the requirements.

Grace: I find 90% of TV commercials annoying. They appear like every 15 minutes during an episode.

Andy: I am okay with these commercials. They pay for the show I want to watch.

Grace: I guess they have to sell their products, but advertising every 15 minutes is too much.

Andy: There are actually some great ones, entertaining and smartly produced.

Grace: But most of them are simply boring. Some only repeat one sentence or two time and time again.

Andy: See, they get your attention. And that's the point.

Grace: But I hate them. And the volume is even louder for the commercials.

Andy: Well, sometimes the commercial break just gives me a chance to get a drink or go to the bathroom. And you can always switch to another channel.

Situation Three

Listen to the dialogue twice and finish the task according to the requirement.

Mark: Hey, isn't that the same jacket advertised by Beckham?

Andy: But he would have bigger pockets to hold all the money paid for the ad.

Mark: You are just jealous. He is so cool in the jacket. I want one like this.

Andy: You make me sick. He may even not wear it.

Mark: You never can tell. Well, why do many companies often name celebrities as their spokesperson? And they pay the spokesperson tons of money.

Andy: That's because they believe celebrity effect can give them more money back.

Mark: But some researchers show that celebrity ads do not always work.

Andy: I guess they just chose the wrong celeb. The biggest doesn't mean the best. Still many people are influenced by celeb advertised products because of their credibility.

Situation Four

Listen to the following short passage twice and finish the task according to the requirement.

Celebrities are people who enjoy public recognition by a large number of people. A customer's buying behavior is hugely influenced by famous people. Marketing experts analyzes the lifestyle of the celebrities to properly assign them to the brand which depicts them perfectly. Their fashion sense, appeal, awareness, fame and public image are reviewed thoroughly to assign them the right charity work or product.

Today, nearly twenty percent of the advertising industry utilizes celebrity endorsement. A celebrity is bound to endorse many products and brands over a course of time. Each time a different image of the celebrity is being projected to the public. The company should keep in mind the previous identity and play accordingly. Projecting a different person every time will sustain the interest of the customers, but at the same time the two identities shouldn't conflict with each other. The captain of England soccer team David Beckham has endorsed many products. While advertising for Gillette, his taste for hairstyles was considered and he was given a bald look.

Item Nine

Situation Two

Listen to the dialogue twice and finish the task according to requirements.

Hotel Clerk: Hello. Sunnyside Inn. May I help you?

Man: Yes, I'd like to reserve a room for two on the 21st of March.

Hotel Clerk: Okay. Let me check our books here for a moment. The 21st of May, right?

Man: No. March, not May.

Hotel Clerk: Oh, sorry. Let me see here. Hmmm.

Man: Are you all booked that night?

Hotel Clerk: Well, we do have one suite available, complete with a kitchenette and a sauna bath. And the view of the city is great, too.

Man: How much is that?

Hotel Clerk: It's only $200 dollars, plus a 10% room tax.

Man: Oh, that's a little too expensive for me. Do you have a cheaper room available either on the 20th or the 22nd?

Hotel Clerk: Well, would you like a smoking or a non-smoking room?

Man: Non-smoking, please.

Hotel Clerk: Okay, we do have a few rooms available on the 20th; we're full on the 22nd, unless you want a smoking room.

Man: Well, how much is the non-smoking room on the 20th?

Hotel Clerk: $80 dollars, plus the 10% room tax.

Man: Okay, that'll be fine.

Hotel Clerk: All right. Could I have your name, please?

Man: Yes, Bob Maexner.

Hotel Clerk: How do you spell your last name, Mr. Maexner?

Man: M—A—E—X—N—E—R.

Hotel Clerk: Okay, Mr. Maexner, we look forward to seeing you on March 20th.

Man: Okay. Goodbye.

Situation Three

　　Listen to the following short passage twice and finish the task according to requirements.

Receptionist: Good morning. Can I help you?

Guest: Good morning. I'd like a single room for a week.

Receptionist: Do you have a reservation?

Guest: Yes, I'm Miss White, I phoned last week.

Receptionist: Yes, Miss White! Can I have your passport, please?

Guest: Yes, here you are.

Receptionist: Thank you. Can you fill in this registration form, please?

Guest: Yes, certainly.

Receptionist: Right, here is your key, it's room number 102; it's on the first floor.

Guest: Thank you.

Receptionist: I'll call the porter to help you with your luggage.

Guest: Oh, thank you very much!

Situation Four

Listen to the dialogue twice and finish the task according to requirements.

Female guest: Hello, I'd like to check out. Room 632.

Luke: Certainly, madam. I hope you enjoyed your stay?

Female guest: Yes, thank you. I thought the conference was very well-organized and I really enjoyed the dinner last night. I know you had some problems but I thought your staff coped with them very well indeed. Eh, that young waitress was a model of how to handle difficult customers.

Luke: I'm pleased to hear that. I'll let her know you were impressed.

Female guest: Yes, I was indeed, although not so much with your chef, I am afraid. Oh, his cooking was excellent but he really shouldn't be let out of the kitchen. If that nice waitress hadn't stepped in, he could have started a major row.

Luke: Oh, dear. That's not so good.

Female guest: Anyway, as I said his cooking was fine. And as a whole, I think the conference was a great success, so I'll be reporting that back to our head office in Hong Kong.

Luke: Oh, I see, you...

Female guest: Yes, I was given the brief to take note of how your hotel performed over the whole conference weekend and report back my findings. And I'm pleased to tell you that —on the whole, they were very favorable indeed, one or two minor hiccups excepted.

Luke: Well that's really good news, madam... Oh, here's your bill for the few extras you had. After what you've just said, I'm almost embarrassed to ask, but... er, how would you like to pay for them?

Female guest: Oh, no, that's fine. Put them on my credit card, thanks. Here...

Luke: Thank you. It's just for the papers and the few things from the mini-bar. So... er, here is your receipt. And I'd like to wish you a safe journey home.

Female guest: Oh, yes, but I want to do a bit of sightseeing before I head home. Can I leave my suitcase here and pick it up later?

Luke: Yes, of course. We'll put your bag in our store room.

Female guest: Fine, and could you order me a taxi for later— my train leaves at 7:15 P. M. ?

Luke: Yes, certainly, what time would you like the taxi for? It takes about 15 minutes to get to the main station.

Female guest: Okay, well then let's say at 6:30 P. M.

Luke: Okay, I hope you enjoy the sights and see you later.

Female guest: Bye.

Item Ten

Situation Two

　　Listen to the dialogue twice and finish the task according to requirements.

Mary: How long have you been enjoying the New Year's Concert, Dad?

Dad: Oh, let me think, about more than ten years.

Mary: Wow, so many years. Do you know how many people enjoyed it on the New Year?

Dad: I don't know exactly, but it is said that over 70 countries broadcast the concert.

Marty: Over 70 countries!

Dad: Yes, so the concert not only delights the audiences in Vienna, but also enjoys great international popularity through the world.

Mary: Including you and me, ha! And is it the Philharmonic that always plays the concert?

Dad: Yes, it has long been a Philharmonic tradition at the New Year to present a program consisting of the lively and at the same time nostalgic music from the vast repertoire of the Johann Strauss family and its contemporaries.

Mary: Just for different conductors for each year.

Dad: Yes, and someone says that the concert is an musical ambassador of Austria, to send people all over the world a New Year's greeting in the spirit of hope, friendship and peace.

Situation Three

　　Listen to the following short passage twice and finish the task according to requirements.

Bob: It is December again now; the annual Grammy Awards Ceremony is coming.

Alice: I am looking forward to it, too.

Bob: Although the Grammy is the US award, it now has become one of the most prominent award ceremonies in the world.

Alice: Yes, it is said that Grammy is like Oscar in the music industry, and most of all over the world are very proud of winning the trophy.

Bob: I think so. In fact the Grammy is a variation of the English word "phonograph". And the award cup is like an old phonograph.

Alice: Do you know the history about Grammy?

Bob: I just know that it started in 1950s.

Alice: Yes, the first Grammy Award telecast took place on the night of November
29, 1959.

Bob: So it has the history about 50 years.

Alice: And the Grammy Awards are presented annually by the National Academy
of Recording Arts and Sciences of the US for outstanding achievements in
the music industry.

Situation Four

**Listen to the following short passage twice and finish the tasks according to re-
quirements.**

The Sound of Music, a feature-film musical about a young religious novice
working as a governess who brings music and happiness to a widower's large family, set in Austria during World War II. Released in 1965 and based on real-life e-
vents, this box-office hit earned Academy Awards for best picture, best director,
best film editing, best sound, and best musical score. Julie Andrews stars as
Maria, the novice nun who, on the advice of her Mother Superior, takes a job as a
governess in the household of Captain Von Trapp (played by Christopher Plummer), caring for his seven children, while she considers her vocation. Maria teaches the children to sing, and she and the captain begin to fall in love. When the Nazis invade Austria, Von Trapp and his family, including Maria, flee the country.
The film was an adaptation of the stage show written by Richard Rodgers and Oscar
Hammerstein II and first produced in 1959; the songs include "Do Re Mi" and "My
Favorite Things" are popular till now.

Item Eleven

Situation Two

Listen to the passage twice and finish the task according to requirements.

Job-searching Means

There are various resources that a job seeker can utilize when hunting for a job. Be sure to make use of the job-searching resources and means which are most relevant to the success of your job search. Manage a healthy balance of utilizing each available resource until you can identify with those that specifically assist your career. By making use of all the resources available to you, your job searches are bound to be improved. Now please compare the following job-searching means.

1. On-campus interviewing program

Pros: Easy to publish your resume and let employers find you. Also many employers post jobs, who apply for jobs that interest you. Some of those employers come to campus—200-600 per year.

Cons: Not every industry or type of job is represented. Driven by the economy (Career Services can't make employers recruit on campus!) OCI has early deadlines and is competitive.

2. Job listings online

Pros: You can view them at 2:00 A. M. if you feel like it. You can view lots of sites and listings without moving your bottom.

Cons: Not every industry or type of job is represented. Web-hunting is not about finding jobs instantly. You need patience to navigate a variety of sites and read listings.

3. Job listings in print

Pros: You'll find some jobs that you won't find online. Some employers have nice printed literature or posters that tell you the personality of the organization.

Cons: You have to view them where and when they're available; i. e. , Career Services during business hours; bulletin boards and professional publications where and when they're available.

4. Job fairs

Pros: Opportunities to speak with many employers at one time in one space. Many on the VT campus each year; each with different sponsors and focused towards specific majors / colleges / types of hiring. If you research the employers in advance, and that shows when you meet employers, you'll be better positioned to have a good experience.

Cons: Not for the shy and retiring (or the mistakenly confident). You need to make a good impression in person and look prepared. Students who go to fairs without doing research in advance sometimes have a not-so-great experience. You're not necessarily learning about every opportunity in each organization—you are just learning where the major hiring needs are. Once a year events—so don't miss the one(s) you need.

Situation Three

Listen to the passage twice and finish the task according to requirements.
Establishing Goals
By carefully planning your career, you can determine:
- interests and strengths;
- short-term objectives and long-term goals;
- education needed;
- occupations that match your skills and interests;
- corporate culture and values that will be right for you;
- future lifestyle.

Think of establishing your goals as a three-step process: self-reflection, self-assessment, and career orientation.

1. Self-reflection

Self-reflection involves thinking about personal characteristics, such as values, and how you fit into the world. These values determine how you behave and what you think is important and influence your relationships and your career path.

2. Self-assessment

Self-assessment requires that you evaluate your abilities and interests in the light of your career goal. Do you have the interests and aptitudes for the work you have chosen? How can you approach your job to make it satisfying?

3. Career Orientation

How can you stay on the right career path? Developing focused short-term objectives and long-term goals will enable you to develop a career plan that will orient you as you travel to your destination.

Situation Four

Listen to the dialogue twice and finish the task according to requirement.

Interviewer: What kind of person do you think you are?

Interviewee: Well, I am always energetic and enthusiastic. That is my strongest personality.

Interviewer: What are your strengths and weaknesses?

Interviewee: Em, as I have said, I am diligent and industrious. On the other hand, sometimes I'm too hard-working and I put myself under too much pressure to make things perfect.

Interviewer: What qualities would you expect of persons working as a team?

Interviewee: To work in a team, in my opinion, two characteristics are necessary for a person. That is, the person must be cooperative and aggressive.

Interviewer: How do you spend your leisure time?

Interviewee: I like playing games and having sports. They are my favorite hobbies.

Interviewer: So, what kind of sport do you like most?

Interviewee: Oh, it's hard to narrow it down to just one. I mean, I like all kinds of sports, basketball, swimming, bike riding and so on. Maybe it is just the reason why I am so energetic and vigorous.

Item Twelve

Situation Two

Listen to the dialogue twice and finish the task according to requirements.

John: Good morning, Miss Lee. I'm John Martin, the managing assistant.

Rose: Good morning, Mr. Martin. Pleased to meet you.

John: First day at work. Are you feeling a bit nervous?

Rose: Yes, nervous and excited.

John: I can remember how I felt on my first day at work. Well, doing a full-time job as a secretary at a company, you should be quite familiar with office routine.

Rose: I'm quick to pick up what is new to me.

John: I'm sure you'll soon get used to everything. Let me take you around the office and show you where everything is and give you a rough idea of your duties here.

Rose: That will help a lot, Mr. Martin.

John: Come with me, look, the desk with an electric typewriter on is yours. If you need paper or carbon paper you can always get it from that cupboard over there. As you can see, you'll use the typewriter often.

Rose: I see. That's part of my work.

John: This is your filing cabinet and all letters must be filed alphabetically.

Rose: What about the confidential file?

John: Oh, that is kept in the safe. Sometimes when a client comes to see the manager, you will take him into the office and it is essential to be polite all the time.

Rose: I'll remember that. Will I have to do anything with samples?

John: No. We have a special samples department.

Rose: Any accounting work?

John: No, that is all done in the accounts department. By the way, are you good at shorthand? You know sometimes you have to take notes in shorthand. I think that is part of the course, too.

Rose: Yes. I came top in shorthand class in the last three examinations.

John: In that case, you must be very good indeed. Last but not least, remember you must come to the office before 9, and you cannot leave until 5:30. Hope you enjoy your work here and we're pleased to have you with us.

Rose: I'm really looking forward to working here. Thank you, Mr. Martin.

Situation Three

Listen to the following short passage twice and finish the task according to requirements.

Janet: Hey! Peter! I can hardly believe it!

Peter: It's you. Janet... Janet Adams! And here we are in Shanghai. What a coincidence!

Janet: What are you doing here? On business trip?

Peter: I work here, as a computer technician at Schuller's Company. What about you?

Janet: Oh, I'm here on holiday for three days. Well, Peter, can you tell me a little about your current job?

Peter: Certainly. What would you like to know?

Janet: What do your responsibilities include?

Peter: I'm responsible for system administration and in-house programming.

Janet: What sort of problems do you deal with on a day-to-day basis?

Peter: Oh, there are always lots of small system problems. I also provide information on a need-to-know basis for employees.

Janet: Thanks for all the information, Peter. It sounds like you have an interesting job.

Peter: Yes, it's very interesting, but stressful, too! What about you? You haven't said anything about yourself.

Janet: I got a job right after graduation, in Beijing, working for a travel agency, as a tourist guide.

Peter: Wow, a nice job, you must have traveled to many places. And would you like to say something about your responsibilities?

Janet: As a tourist guide, I must be responsible for arranging and coordinating tour activities, and offering service of transportation, accommodations, sightseeing, shopping and entertainment. It's a demanding and tiring job, but a rewarding job, too. I love it.

Peter: Glad you're doing what you like now. Nice to meet you again. Hope to keep in touch with you.

Janet: So do I.

Situation Four

Listen to the following short passages twice and finish the task according to requirements.

This delightful pull along wood toy has a tail that wags, eyes that roll and a tongue that swings from side to side. His ears can be rotated and his head jiggles as he is pulled along on his rubber trimmed wheels. Browny comes nicely boxed and makes it a fabulous special occasion or first birthday gift for both boys and girls. The price is $34.

Another attractive baby gift, this gorgeous little wooden toy pulled along is just the thing to accompany babies and toddlers on journeys about the house. We love droopy ears and the bell (hidden safely inside) that softly tinkles when he is on the move. Hand made, hand-painted and beautifully packaged. The price is $32.

Item Thirteen

Situation Two

Listen to the dialogue twice and finish the task according to requirements.

Susan: OK. Let's review our start-up plans. When do you think we'll be able to move into our new office?

Helen: But moving in and actually getting started are two different things. Well, we can move in any time after July 1st.

Susan: Good point. Anyway, I have you helping out with purchasing new equipment. Can you do that?

Helen: As a matter of fact, I practically ran my last company—from marketing to finance.

Susan: There should be no problem, then. Also, I'm looking forward to reading your marketing plan. When will you hand it to me?

Helen: Next Monday. By the way, have you begun to investigate factories?

Susan: Yes, I've started, and I've found some good people for R and D. Oh, by the way, the art people called to discuss the design of our logos.

Helen: Oh, no! Millions of details: logos, slogans, a letterhead, business cards...

Susan: And you thought setting up a company was going to be easy?

Situation Three

Listen to the following short passage twice and finish the task according to requirements.

How should we know what we really want to do? Between our dream and goal, there are too many different options. If you work hard, you may get your goal, but a dream doesn't always come true. We must know our goals clearly, do what we want, and study harder than before, to get ready for every chance the god has given us. Everyone needs personal development. I believe that life is like the weather: we can't know what will happen next; maybe it will rain or be a sunny day, or even it might storm, but we can do something for ourselves, we can make plans for our future to let our future more successful.

Situation Four

Listen to the following short passage twice and finish the task according to requirements.

I'm studying personal development now. I benefit a lot from this course, and it lets me know how to develop my life in the right way. Firstly, we should have self-confidence, have goals, positive attitudes, good communication, and so on. Accompanying the economic development, society needs more and more pluralism talents. We must prepare ourselves to adapt to the environment around us. Survival of the fittest, it is like a game. If you can't fit the requirements of society, you must get out of the game.

I will match my personality with my career goals, and make a plan. My goal is to be a successful business woman, and have my own company. But, this goal is very hard to me now, so I need more knowledge, and I need to realize my interest, ability, characteristic to unite the practice. Try my best to do everything well.

Item Fourteen

Situation Two

Listen to the dialogue twice and finish the task according to requirements.

M: Excuse me. Is this the Business Department of ICBC?

W: Yes. What can I do for you?

M: I want to deposit some money in your bank.

W: Which would you like, fixed deposit or current deposit?

M: Current deposit.

W: How much are you going to place to your credit?

M: 2,000 Yuan.

W: Please fill out a deposit slip. Write down your account number, name and amount.

M: OK.

W: Would you please hand me your passbook with the deposit slip?

M: Here you are.

W: Please input your secret code.

M: Is that all right?

W: That's good. Here is your passbook with the check slip. Please check it.

M: There are no problems. Thank you.

W: You are welcome.

Situation Three

　　Listen to the dialogue twice and finish the task according to requirements.

M: Hello!

W: Hello! Is that Mr. Ford?

M: Yes, that's he. Who's that?

W: Miss Green speaking. I want to buy stocks.

M: What stock do you want to buy and how many?

W: I want to buy 1,000 shares of Lenovo.

M: Let me get the asking price of the stock. I'll tell you a minute later.

W: OK.

Situation Four

　　Listen to the passage twice and finish the tasks according to requirements.

　　When you buy insurance, you enter into a written agreement with the insurance company. This agreement is called a policy. The person who buys insurance is the policyholder. According to the agreement, the insurance company promises to pay the policyholder if certain types of losses occur. The policy states exactly what losses the company will pay for. For this protection, the policyholder makes regular payments to the insurance company. Each payment is called a premium.

Item Fifteen

Situation Two

Listen to the dialogue twice and finish the task according to requirements.

Wang Qian: How many people are in your family?

Zhang Lin: As you know, China has a single-child policy. Therefore, there's just my husband, my daughter and I. What about in your family?

Wang Qian: I have one daughter and one son. Then there's my husband and I. What about your parents? Do they live with your family?

Zhang Lin: Not any more. They live with my brother now. And yours?

Wang Qian: My parents live by themselves now. When they get older, they'll probably go to a retirement home. Do you just have one brother?

Zhang Lin: No, I have two older brothers and one younger sister. What about you?

Wang Qian: I also grew up in a big family. I have one older brother and three younger sisters.

Zhang Lin: How long have you been married?

Wang Qian: About seven years now. And you?

Zhang Lin: I've been married for about five years. What do you think about divorce?

Wang Qian: It's becoming more and more common. However, I don't ever want to get divorced myself! What about you?

Zhang Lin: If my husband cheated on me or treated me badly, I would get a divorce.

Wang Qian: If that happens, maybe you could marry my brother and we could become in-laws!

Zhang Lin: (ha, ha) I'll keep that in mind, but don't tell my husband.

Wang Qian: Of course not!

Situation Three

Listen to the dialogue twice and finish the task according to requirements.

Mary: How are your wedding plans going?

Lucy: Very well. We started organizing everything early to avoid a last minute rush to get things done. The only thing that isn't ready yet is my wedding dress.

Mary: When will that be ready?

Lucy: The dressmakers said that it would be ready in two weeks.

Mary: You're getting married in three weeks. So that should be OK. So, you've prepared the church, catering, transport, hotel—everything.

Lucy: Yes. We've taken care of all of that. We decided not to get married in a church though. Neither of us is very religious.

Mary: Which hotel will the reception be held at?

Lucy: The Holiday Inn. They're taking care of the catering, including the wedding cake. I'm sure they'll do a good job.

Mary: Oh, yes. It's an excellent hotel. A friend of mine had her wedding reception there and said it was perfect, though very expensive.

Lucy: Yes. It will be expensive, but we think it will be worth. It gives us great peace of mind to know that our reception is in the hands of experienced people.

Mary: I think you make the right decision.

Situation Four

Listen to the passage twice and finish the task according to requirements.

A couple were driving to a church to get married. On the way, they got into a car accident and died. When they arrive in heaven, they see St. Peter at the gate. They ask him if he could arrange it, so they could marry in heaven. St. Peter tells them that he'll do his best to work on it for them. Three months pass by and the couple hear nothing. They bump into St. Peter and ask him about the marriage. He says, "I'm still working on it." Two years pass by and no marriage. St. Peter again assures them that he's working on it. Finally after twenty long years, St. Peter comes running with a priest and tells the couple it's time for their wedding. The couple marry and live happily for a while. But after a few months the couple go and find St. Peter and tell him things are not working out, and that they want to get a divorce. "Can you arrange it for us?" they ask. St. Peter replies, "Are you kidding? It took me twenty years to find a priest up here. How am I gonna find you a lawyer?"

Words & Expressions

Item	Words & Expressions	
1	caterpillar	毛虫
1	insurmountable	不能克服的,难以对付的
1	nectar	花蜜
1	puzzled	困惑的
1	secretary	文秘,秘书
1	stimulate	刺激,激励,鼓舞
1	treatment	对待,处理
1	apartment	一套公寓房间
1	frown	皱眉
1	furious	狂怒的,猛烈的
1	harmoniously	和谐地
1	honey-comb	蜂窝
1	impatient	不耐烦的,急躁的
1	initial	开始的
1	unwilling to answer	不愿意回答
2	additive	添加剂
2	administration	行政,行政机关
2	colon	结肠,直肠
2	courtesy	礼貌,好意,恩惠
2	credit	信用,荣誉,贷款,学分;归功于,赞颂,信任
2	decline	拒绝,衰微,跌落/降低,婉谢
2	dessert	甜食
2	economic	经济的,经济学的
2	efficient	效率高的,有能力的
2	enormous	巨大的,庞大的
2	entertainment	娱乐
2	grace	优雅,雅致,魅力,恩惠,慈悲
2	income	收入,所得

2	insignificant	无关紧要的,可忽略的
2	list	目录,名单,明细表;列出,列于表上,记入名单内
2	nitrate	硝酸盐
2	nitrite	亚硝酸盐
2	obtain	获得,得到;通用,流行,存在
2	penicillin	青霉素
2	pepper	胡椒粉
2	profound	极深的,深厚的
2	prone	易于……的,有……倾向的
2	receipt	收据
2	recommend	建议,推荐,劝告,介绍
2	repeatedly	重复地,再三地
2	specialty	专门,特别,特性
2	steak	牛排
2	unfit	不合适的
2	tremendously	惊人地
2	balanced diet	均衡饮食
2	be prone to	倾向于
2	be related to	和……有关的
2	benefit a lot from...	从……中获益
2	credit card	信用卡
2	have effects on	产生影响
2	make enormous steps	有了巨大的进步
2	on a diet	节食
2	provide sb. with	向某人提供
2	play an important role	扮演着重要角色
3	annual	一年的;一年一次的;年度的
3	appeal	呼吁,恳求;有吸引力;上诉
3	approach	接近,靠近;方法,方式
3	billboard	广告牌
3	buff	迷,爱好者
3	canyon	(既长又深,谷底常有溪流的)峡谷
3	concept	概念,观念,思想
3	conservation	(对自然资源的)保护,管理

3	cruise	巡航;航游;(坐船)旅行
3	departure	离开;出发,启程
3	eagle	鹰
3	extinguish	熄灭,灭绝,偿清
3	fantastic	奇异的;古怪的;极好的,了不起的
3	horrible	可怕的,令人毛骨悚然的
3	immigrant	(外来)移民,侨民
3	journey	旅行;旅程,行程
3	luxurious	奢侈的;骄奢淫逸的;豪华的
3	meadow	草地,牧草地
3	nest	巢;窝;穴
3	numerous	许多的,很多的
3	recommendation	推荐;推荐信,介绍信
3	refreshing	提神的;清凉的;使人耳目一新的
3	resort	常去的休闲度假之处;名胜
3	stove	火炉,暖炉
3	territory	领土,版图;领地;领域,范围
3	uncommon	不寻常的;罕见的;非凡的,杰出的
3	witness	见证,目击;作……的证人;目击者;见证人
3	wonder	纳闷;想知道;惊奇,惊叹;奇迹;奇观
3	as easy as pie	极容易,小菜一碟
3	historical site	历史古迹
3	jet airplane	喷气式飞机
3	lecture hall	演讲厅;大讲堂
3	natural wonder	自然奇观
3	return journey	往返旅行
3	scenic spot	风景区
3	tourist attraction	令人向往的旅游胜地;观光胜地
3	travel agency	旅行社
3	Yellow Crane Tower	黄鹤楼
4	love	(网球)零分
4	courtyard	院子,庭院
4	appear	出现
4	baseball	棒球

4	bowling	保龄球
4	championship	锦标赛,冠军称号
4	completely	完全地
4	couch	长沙发
4	court	球场
4	create	创造
4	deuce	(还要继续比赛下去的)局末平分,盘末平分
4	devoted	挚爱的,忠诚的
4	director	董事
4	fit	健康的
4	glue	胶水,黏在……上
4	gymnasium	体育馆,健身房
4	hockey	冰球
4	household	家庭的
4	influence	影响
4	jog	慢跑
4	kid	开玩笑,取笑
4	monk	修道士
4	occupy	占据
4	pond	池塘
4	professional	职业的
4	racquetball	壁球
4	religion	宗教
4	revel	沉迷于,狂欢
4	rink	溜冰场
4	scoring	计分,得分
4	sideline	旁线,侧道
4	spectator	观众,旁观者
4	stuff	东西
4	surfing	冲浪
4	toiletry	化妆品
4	tournament	锦标赛,联赛
4	weightlifting	举重
4	widow	寡妇
4	hallowed ground	圣地

4	scuba diving	潜水
4	board of directors	董事会
4	couch potato	因长久坐在沙发上看电视不活动而发胖的人
4	ice-skating	滑冰
4	live up to	不辜负
4	take delight in	以……为乐
5	contagious	传染性的,会蔓延的,会传播的
5	contradict	同……抵触
5	exaggerate	夸大,夸张
5	filtration	过滤,筛选
5	gauze	薄纱,纱布,金属网
5	influenza	流行性感冒,流感
5	insomnia	失眠
5	leaching	滤去
5	municipal	市政的,地方性的
5	pollutant	污染物
5	symptom	症状,征兆
5	vaccine	疫苗
5	virus	病毒
5	A/H1N1 flu	甲型 H1N1 流感
5	blow up	爆炸
5	stuff up	塞住
6	addiction	沉溺,上瘾
6	adventure	冒险,奇遇;大胆进行
6	browser	浏览器,吃嫩叶的动物,浏览书本的人
6	convenient	方便的
6	correspondence	相应,通信,信件
6	dealer	商人
6	decade	十年
6	destination	目的地
6	economical	节俭的,经济的,合算的
6	explosion	爆发,扩张

6	fingertip	指尖
6	hone	磨炼,用磨刀石磨
6	impact	冲击,冲突,影响;挤入;撞击,对……发生影响
6	inhale	吸入
6	instant	立即,瞬间;立即的,即时的
6	mar	损毁,损伤,糟蹋
6	mushroom	迅速生长,迅速增加
6	mutual	共同的,相互的
6	negative	否定的,负的,消极的;底片,页数;否定
6	nephew	侄子,外甥
6	option	选择
6	overwhelming	势不可挡的,压倒的
6	positive	肯定的,积极的,绝对的;正面的,正数的,阳性的
6	respondent	回答的,应答的,感应的;应答者
6	synchronous	同时的,同步的
6	trap	圈套,陷阱;设圈套,设陷阱
6	unscrupulous	肆无忌惮的,无天理的
6	virtual	虚拟的,实质的
7	accompany	陪伴,陪着;陪衬,伴随
7	accounting	会计;会计学
7	certification	证书
7	childhood	儿童期,童年时代,早年
7	counselor	顾问;律师;法律顾问
7	definitely	明确(确切)地
7	diploma	毕业文凭,学位证书
7	dramatize	渲染;使戏剧化
7	imaginary	想象中的,假想的;虚构的
7	infinite	无限的;无极的;无限扩展的;无边际的
7	lifelong	终身的;毕生的

7	marketable	可销售的；适于市场上销售的；有销路的
7	occupational	职业(性)的
7	pension	养老金，退休金
7	plunge	使陷入，使遭受
7	realistic	现实主义(者)的
7	retirement	退休
7	tuition	学费
7	welfare	福利事业
7	career-oriented	以就业为目标
8	assign	分配，分派；派定，指定，选派
8	bald	秃顶的；无草木的；赤裸裸的；无装饰的，单调的
8	celebrity	名人，名流；名声，著名
8	charity	博爱，慈善；施舍；善举；慈善团体
8	conflict	矛盾，冲突，斗争
8	credibility	可信性，确实性
8	depict	描画，雕出；描述，描写
8	endorsement	背书；赞同，支持；宣传
8	grab	攫取，抓取；夺取，霸占；将……吸引住，影响
8	identity	身份，本体；同一
8	informative	情报的；见闻广博的；教育性的，有益的
8	jealous	妒忌的；吃醋的
8	project	计划，规划；投射(光线等)，投映
8	sustain	支撑，承受；维持，供养；忍受，禁得起
8	thorough	彻底的，完全的；十分仔细的
8	utilize	利用
9	albeit	虽然；即使
9	amenity	适意，温和，礼仪，怡人
9	available	可用的，可得到的，有用的，有效的
9	blunder	失策，绊倒，弄糟

9	blur	使……模糊,弄脏
9	complimentary	问候的,称赞的,夸奖的,免费赠送的
9	favorabble	有利的,赞许的,良好的,顺利的,偏祖的
9	hiccup	打嗝,暂时性的小问题
9	kitchenette	小厨房
9	lavish	大方的,丰富的,浪费的
9	recreational	休闲的,娱乐的
9	sauna	桑拿浴,蒸汽浴
9	segment	划分
9	suite	随员,套房,一组
9	tub	桶,浴盆
9	check in	登记
10	album	集邮本,照相簿,唱片簿
10	ambassador	大使,使节
10	beat	打,敲打声,拍子
10	burial	埋葬,葬礼,坟墓
10	campfire	营火,篝火
10	ceremony	典礼,仪式,礼节,礼仪
10	chantey	船歌
10	chorus	合唱队,歌舞队;合唱
10	circus	广场,马戏团,马戏表演,竞技场
10	congregation	集合,会合
10	contemporary	同时代人,同龄人
10	crown	王冠,王权;使……成王,加冕,居……之顶
10	governess	女家庭教师
10	household	家庭的,家喻户晓的
10	hymn	赞美诗,圣歌;唱赞美歌
10	mournful	悲恸的,悲哀的,令人惋惜的
10	musical	音乐片;音乐的
10	nostalgic	乡愁的;怀旧的
10	novice	新信徒,新手
10	nun	尼姑,修女
10	Oscar	奥斯卡(男子名),奥斯卡金像奖

10	philharmonic	爱好音乐的，交响乐团的
10	phonograph	留声机，电唱机
10	priest	教士，神父
10	prominent	杰出的,显著的,突出的
10	repertoire	全部节目，保留剧目
10	serenade	为……弹奏或歌唱小夜曲
10	spectacle	值得看的东西，光景，眼镜
10	talent	才能，人才，天资
10	telecast	以电视广播传送；电视广播
10	trophy	奖品，战利品
10	variation	变化,变动,变种,变奏曲
10	virtuoso	演奏家演艺精湛的人
10	widower	鳏夫
10	worshiper	崇拜者，礼拜者
10	box-office	票房
10	fall in love	陷入爱河,爱上
10	play an important part in	在……中起重要作用
10	provide. . . for. . .	供给,为……作准备
10	seek to	追求,争取,设法
10	the Nazis	纳粹
10	the Vienna Philharmonic New Year's Concert	维也纳新年音乐会
11	abuse	滥用,辱骂,虐待
11	acknowledge	承认,告知收悉,答谢,报偿
11	aggressive	积极进取的；活泼的;侵略的;攻击的;挑衅的
11	alternate	交替的,轮流的;预备的,候补的
11	appeal	恳求,诉请,上诉,吸引力
11	appliance	器具，设备，装置，仪表，器械，附件
11	assessment	评估
11	attorney	辩护律师
11	characteristic	特性,特征,特色;特性的,特有的,有特色的
11	conflicting	抵触的,冲突的,矛盾的,不相容的

11	cooperative	合作的，协作的，共同的
11	demonstrate	表示，表明；举例说明；证实
11	despair	绝望，失望，悲观
11	determine	决心，决意；确定；限定，规定
11	diligent	勤勉的；刻苦的，勤奋的
11	diploma	文凭，毕业证书
11	energetic	精力充沛的，充满活力的，精神饱满的
11	enthusiastic	热心的，热情的；热烈的
11	haphazardly	偶然地，随意地
11	impasse	难局，僵局，死路，死胡同
11	implement	完成，实施
11	industrious	勤劳的，刻苦的，奋发的
11	integrity	诚实，正直，廉正
11	lapse	堕落，减退，消失，流逝
11	manufacturer	制造商，厂主；制造厂
11	negativity	否定性，消极性
11	occupation	职业；占领，占据；占有
11	orientation	定位；取向
11	outright	公开地；直率地；坦白地，露骨地
11	paddle	桨，划桨；划桨，戏水，涉水
11	percentage	百分比，比率
11	permanent	永久性的，耐久的，固定不变的
11	priority	优先，重点；优先权；次序；轻重缓急
11	privilege	特权，优惠，特殊的荣幸
11	prod	刺针，刺棒，激励话，提醒物；戳，刺，刺激
11	prolong	拉长；延长；引伸；拖延，延期
11	reflection	反映，反射；沉思，反省，思考
11	reputation	名声；名誉
11	snag	障碍物，意外障碍；造成阻碍，清除障碍物
11	strategically	在战略上，颇有策略地
11	temporary	暂时的，临时的；一时的
12	accommodation	住处，膳宿

12	alphabetically	按字母表顺序地
12	appliance	器具,器械,装置
12	budget	预算
12	cabinet	陈列柜
12	catalogue	目录,总目
12	committee	委员会
12	commodity	商品,日用品
12	confidential	机密的,易于信任他人的
12	coincidence	巧合
12	coordinate	协调,整合,综合
12	corporate	法人 ,公司
12	cupboard	橱柜
12	demanding	要求多的,吃力的
12	document	文件,公文
12	enterprise	企业,事业
12	entertainment	娱乐
12	essential	必要的,重要的,本质的
12	expand	使……膨胀,扩张
12	fabulous	传说的,难以置信的,好极了
12	finance	财政,财务
12	gorgeous	华丽的,灿烂的,好极了
12	gratitude	感激之情
12	implement	实现,执行,使……生效
12	inquiry	询问,询价,调查,查问
12	jiggle	轻摇,微动
12	laptop	手提电脑
12	laser	激光
12	logo	图形,商标
12	mechanical	机械的,力学的,呆板的
12	moderate	适度的,稳健的,温和的,中等的
12	negotiate	商议,谈判,交涉
12	nutritious	有营养成分的,营养的
12	organisation	组织(团体,有机体)
12	photocopier	复印机
12	projector	投影机
12	purchase	购买,购买的物品

12	reframe	再构造(给……装上新框架)
12	represent	代表,表现,表示,描绘
12	representative	代表,众议员,典型
12	responsibility	责任
12	restore	回复,恢复,归还
12	rotate	(使)旋转
12	routine	例行公事,常规
12	savor	加调味品于,使有风味,尽情享受
12	scanner	扫描机,扫描盘,光电子扫描装置
12	shareholder	股东
12	shorthand	速记
12	shredder	碎纸机
12	stationery	文具
12	strategy	战略,策略
12	stressful	紧张的,压力大的
12	tinkle	发出叮叮的声响
12	toddler	初学走路的孩子
12	transportation	运输,运输系统,运输工具
12	wag	摇摆
12	be alert	警觉,留心
12	be capable of doing	能做
12	be responsible for	负责
12	day-to-day basis	按每日
12	need-to-know basis	按需要
12	pick up	学会
13	budding	萌芽的,发育的,少壮的
13	accompany	陪伴,伴奏
13	appropriately	适当地,恰如其分地,恰当地,合适地
13	block	障碍,阻塞,妨碍;(时间的)一段
13	capitalize	以大写字母写,资本化;转作资本
13	entrepreneur	企业家;创业者
13	flounder	(在水中)挣扎,困难地往前走,蹒跚,发慌
13	foundation	建立,创建;基础,基本原理;地基

13	franchise	公民权；选举权；参政权；特权，特许
13	franchisor	授予特许者
13	inspiration	灵感
13	interview	接见，会见
13	interviewee	被接见者，被访问者
13	interviewer	会见者
13	investigate	研究；调查；勘测；试验；研究；审查
13	moderator	仲裁者，调停者
13	niche	合适的环境，活动
13	odds	可能性，可能的机会
13	option	选择；选择权；选择自由
13	realistic	现实的，逼真的，现实主义的，实在论的
13	registration	登记；登记证；登记人员的数目；注册
13	saturated	充满了……的；浸透的，湿透的，浸透的
13	schedule	时间表，课程表，日程表；火车时刻表
13	scheme	计划，规划，方案，设计；安排；办法
13	simultaneously	同时地
13	stream	一连串，接二连三，源源不断（的事情）
13	survival	生存，幸存，残存；幸存者；残存物，残存的风俗
13	adapt to	适合
13	check in	登记，报到
13	check out	结账
13	Confucian Temple	孔夫子庙
13	end up	结束
13	jacks of all trades	万事通
13	Lingyin Temple	灵隐寺
13	opening ceremony	开幕仪式
13	pick up	接人

13	pluralism talent	复合人才
13	scope out	仔细研究
13	subscribing to	订阅
13	under auspices of	由……单位主办
13	welcome and opening address by	由……致欢迎词
13	Zhongshan Museum	中山陵
14	account	户头，账目
14	advisable	适当的，可取的；合理的
14	agent	代理人，经纪人；代理商
14	bond	债券，公债，公司债
14	browse	浏览，吃草
14	code	密码，电码；代码；代号
14	conservative	保守的，稳健的
14	crisis	危机，恐慌，危险期
14	currency	通货，货币
14	current	流通的，现在的，当前的，流行的
14	deposit	储蓄，贮存
14	emergency	突然事件；紧急情况，
14	inflation	胀大，夸张，通货膨胀
14	insurance	保险（业）
14	interest	利息，息金
14	memo	备忘录
14	minimize	减到最少；按最小（值 或限度）
14	passbook	银行存折
14	policy	政策，保险单
14	potential	可能的；潜在的
14	premium	保险费
14	principal	主要的，最重要的，首要的
14	recommendation	推荐，介绍；建议
14	security	有价证券
14	share	股份
14	slip	插条
14	stability	稳定（性）
14	stock	股份总额，股本，股票
14	unique	唯一的，独特的

14	volatile	易变的，短暂的；非永久性的
14	withdrawal	提款，撤退，退回
14	a written agreement	书面协议
14	account number and amount	账号和数量
14	Business Department of ICBC	中国工商银行营业部
14	check slip	对账单
14	fill out a deposit slip	填写存款单
14	fixed deposit or current deposit	定期或活期存款
14	input your secret code	输入密码
14	pay for losses	赔付损失
14	real estate	不动产；房地产
14	set aside	留出，不顾，取消，驳回
14	asking price of the stock	股票报价
14	treasury bonds	财政长期债券，库存公司债
15	divorce	离婚，脱离，使离婚，与……脱离
15	idiot	白痴，愚人，傻瓜
15	committee	委员会
15	essential	本质的，实质的，基本的，提炼的，精华的；本质，实质，要素
15	extension	延长，扩充，范围；[逻]外延的，客观现实的
15	grip	紧握，紧夹，掌握，控制，把手，抓住
15	occupy	占，占用，占领，占据
15	pregnant	怀孕的，重要的，富有意义的，孕育的
15	resident	居民；居住的，常驻的
15	responsibility	责任，职责
15	romantic	传奇式的，浪漫的，空想的，夸大的
15	sweat	汗；(使)出汗
15	trifle	琐事，少量，蛋糕，小事，开玩笑，玩弄，浪费，嘲弄